IMAGES O

THE AMERICANS FROM THE ARDENNES TO VE DAY

RARE PHOTOGRAPHS FROM WARTIME ARCHIVES

Brooke Blades

Pen & Sword
MILITARY

First published in Great Britain in 2020 by
PEN & SWORD MILITARY
An imprint of
Pen & Sword Books Ltd
47 Church Street
Barnsley
South Yorkshire
S70 2AS

ISBN 978-1-52676-608-3

Typeset by Concept, Huddersfield, West Yorkshire HD4 5JL
Printed and bound in England by CPI Group (UK) Ltd, Croydon, CR0 4YY

Pen & Sword Books Limited incorporates the imprints of Atlas, Archaeology, Aviation, Discovery, Family History, Fiction, History, Maritime, Military, Military Classics, Politics, Select, Transport, True Crime, Air World, Frontline Publishing, Leo Cooper, Remember When, Seaforth Publishing, The Praetorian Press, Wharncliffe Local History, Wharncliffe Transport, Wharncliffe True Crime and White Owl.

For a complete list of Pen & Sword titles please contact
PEN & SWORD BOOKS LIMITED
47 Church Street, Barnsley, South Yorkshire S70 2AS, England
E-mail: enquiries@pen-and-sword.co.uk
Website: www.pen-and-sword.co.uk

Contents

Acknowledgements

This third volume completes the story of the Americans in the campaign to end the Second World War in north-west Europe. The narrative and images provide details of the struggle from the surprise Ardennes offensive launched in December 1944 to the time when the guns ceased firing in early May 1945. The efforts of all American armies are not covered. The essential contributions of allies from Britain, Canada, France, Poland and other nations are recognized. In a departure from the series title, the final chapter in part addresses the service of millions of soldiers from Russia and other countries in the defeat of Nazi Germany on the Eastern Front.

I have benefited much from the work of many historians but owe a special debt to John Keegan and Charles MacDonald. Both wrote with compassion and humanity. Mr Keegan quite simply changed the manner in which people think about the experience of war, while never losing his moral perspective. Mr MacDonald was an infantry company commander in north-west Europe who brought the knowledge of those experiences to his writings.

I am most grateful to Henry Wilson and Matt Jones at Pen & Sword Ltd for supporting the effort in such a kind manner while exhibiting considerable patience during preparation of the manuscript. Tara Moran is a marketing wizard and Lori Jones provided support in things logistical. The editors Barnaby Blacker and Noel Sadler have improved the manuscript in more ways than can be mentioned and for this I extend my sincere appreciation. My wife Meg and our daughter Emma offered sustained encouragement and interest in the series of illustrated volumes.

Lillian and John Leary provided a photograph of John's father; it was an honour to tell something of his story. Joe French from the Commonwealth War Graves Commission willingly assisted me by providing a photograph. My friend Pawel Valde-Nowak kindly provided a translation of the wall plaque in Kraków.

Gratitude is once again extended to Holly Reed, Kaitlyn Crain Enriquez and Sarah Lepianka in Still Pictures, Andrew Knight in Cartography and Stanley Fanaras in the General Records room of the National Archives in College Park, Maryland. As has been the case throughout the series, Julie Cressman prepared the maps that enhance the presentation of this volume.

Columbia University Press granted permission for use of an important quotation from *Assassins of Memory* by Pierre Vidal-Naquet. The Center of Military History was equally kind in allowing use of maps and map information from official histories by Hugh Cole and Charles MacDonald.

This book is dedicated to my very good friends Jehanne Féblot-Augustins and Georges Augustins in France and friends who shared their memories of service in the 17th Airborne Division: Herbert Anderson, Ed Ballas, Ralph Clarke, Hal Green, Robert Haight, Irv Hennings, John Kormann and Stanley Morrison.

Strafford, Pennsylvania
June 2019

Chapter One

The Winter Offensive

On 17 December 1944, the second day of the Ardennes winter offensive, Dwight Eisenhower convened a meeting of his commanders by stating there would be no long faces at the table. Senior army leaders realized that their superiority in men and quantities of equipment, particularly air power, would eventually determine the outcome. Nevertheless, the eternal optimist George Patton recorded in a dark moment it was still possible for the Allies to lose the war. Over the next six weeks, the offensive was halted with great loss of life to the Germans. However, more American soldiers were killed, wounded or declared missing than in any other battle in the history of the nation.

In mid-December 1944 the Germans launched an offensive planned since mid-September on the express orders of Hitler. The advance by three armies fell upon a portion of the overextended American First Army in the Ardennes in eastern Belgium and Luxembourg. Two American divisions – the 106th that arrived only a few days earlier and the battered 28th – resisted but were overrun and severely reduced. Other divisions sustained heavy casualties but held due to defence in depth and massive artillery support. Lieutenant Colonel Derrill Daniel told new soldiers in the 2nd Battalion 26th Infantry who arrived near Bütgenbach – replacements for those lost a few weeks earlier at Merode on the edge of the Hürtgen Forest – that the battalion would establish a line from which there would be no retreat.

One armoured column from the 1st SS Panzer Division under command of Obersturmbannführer Joachim Peiper broke through the initial line of defence and pushed west in an effort to reach the River Meuse and beyond. In their wake they left a trail of murdered American soldiers south of Malmédy and Belgian civilians in several towns. The column was eventually halted by terrain, bridges destroyed by stalwart combat engineers and defensive lines formed by the 30th Division and 82nd Airborne Division.

* * *

The Offensive

German planning began in the summer and early autumn of 1944 following the fall of Antwerp to the Allies. The thrust was to be a powerful one with the goal of reaching

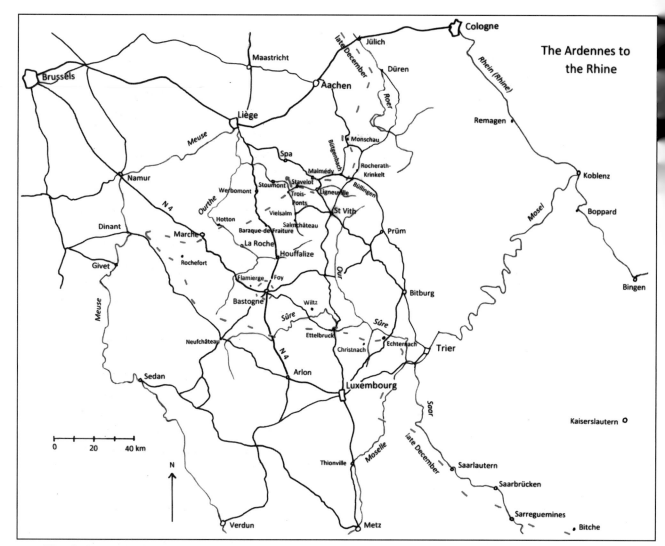

The Ardennes to the Rhine.

Antwerp. If successful, British/Canadian forces in the Second Army and at least one American army in the north would be isolated from the remainder of the Allied armies. Existing armoured and infantry divisions were rebuilt and new *Volks* (people's) infantry divisions were raised. The date on which the offensive would be launched was pushed back to the middle of December. By that time three armies were assembled to crash through the Ardennes south of Aachen and north of Luxembourg City – from north to south, Sixth Panzer Army under Oberstgruppenführer der Waffen-SS Josef 'Sepp' Dietrich, Fifth Panzer Army commanded by General der Panzertruppen Hasso von Manteuffel, and Seventh Army led by General der Panzertruppen Erich Brandenberger. The emphasis on rapid advance beyond the River Meuse was placed on the northern and central armies, both of which had armoured panzer divisions at their disposal. The Seventh Army had no such heavily armoured divisions and was expected to move west to the Meuse and hold a strong line along the southern flank.

Among the lessons Hitler and *Oberkommando der Wehrmacht*, or OKW, derived from previous campaigns, particularly in Normandy, was the seeming inability to maintain an effective armoured reserve to counter Allied attacks. Even when such a force was evidently assembled near Mortain, its striking power was largely negated by the devastating power of Allied air forces (the forewarning offered by Ultra intelligence was as yet unknown to the Germans). As a consequence, the offensive incorporated proposed remedies. Most of the armoured units, particularly the vaunted SS divisions, required extensive rehabilitation after Normandy and were not employed in holding the Siegfried Line positions in the fall. However, the 116th Panzer would fight near Aachen and again in the Hürtgen Forest, while Panzer Lehr Division opposed Third Army units in the Saar. Both divisions sustained considerable losses before the offensive. The armour would be concentrated in the Ardennes to strike an overwhelming blow. In addition, the expected deterioration of weather conditions in mid-December with cloud cover and snow would – it was hoped – prevent the Allied air forces from intervening.[1]

Data from Enigma intercepts, known to the Allies as Ultra, and the apparent disregard for indications in those intercepts that something major was up along the Western Front during the fall of 1944, have not been fully appreciated. Bennett considered numerous other messages warranted more attention: creation of Sixth Panzer Army in September, equipment allocations involving several SS panzer divisions from October onward, train movements westward from November and orders for fighter planes to protect those trains, assembly of other Luftwaffe formations for unspecified reasons, and repeated aerial photography in the northern Ardennes near Malmédy and above crossings of the River Meuse from late November. While acknowledging possible alternative explanations at the time and obvious advantages inherent in post-offensive analyses, the problem for Bennett lay with a fundamental Allied confidence that the Germans were simply incapable of mounting a major offensive. Intelligence projections viewed the movements as attempts to create a strong reserve near the Rhine and thus reflected Allied intentions rather than actual German capabilities described in the messages.[2]

German forces that advanced in the Ardennes were a mixed lot ranging from experienced units to those raised to include young boys and older – sometimes much older – men. All had been partially or almost completely recreated following substantial casualties in Normandy and Belorussia during the summer of 1944.

Demographics for two formations illustrate the variations. The 9th SS Panzer Division fought in Normandy and assisted in extricating encircled Wehrmacht units near Falaise. Transferred to Holland to rest and re-equip, the division's placement near Arnhem proved fortuitous in September during Market Garden. Most prisoners from the division – 73 per cent – in late summer and fall of 1944 traced their origins to Russia and two-thirds were 31 years of age or older. By mid-January 1945, those captured during the offensive reflected more balanced origins – 40 per cent from Russia and 37 per cent from Germany – and ages, with about one-third (35 per cent) older than 30 years and slightly more (38 per cent) 20 years or younger.

The 12th Volksgrenadier Division was essentially eliminated during the massive Russian offensive known as the Destruction of Army Group Centre in the summer of 1944. The unit was rebuilt and sent west to help hold the Siegfried Line before the December offensive. Prisoners from the division remained mostly German in origin (67 to 82 per cent) from 1944 into early 1945. The vast majority of the troops in 1944 – 84 per cent – were evenly divided between those younger than 21 or older than 30. The youngest element dropped to 28 per cent by mid-March 1945 at a time when the oldest cohort still accounted for four of every ten soldiers.[3]

The Northern Flank

The *Schwerpunkt* or point of maximum effort for the overall offensive was along the northern edge under the command of Sepp Dietrich and Sixth Panzer Army. Following an artillery preparation, infantry divisions would advance to overrun American front line positions, with immediate support provided by powerful armoured divisions in two corps. The 1st SS and 12th SS Panzer Divisions moved along parallel routes while 2nd SS and 9th SS Panzer Divisions were available for support and exploitation of initial gains. It was expected the leading armoured units would cross the River Meuse before substantial American reserves could be assembled.

Two American divisions were present at the northern edge and would bear the consequences of the initial attack. The 99th Division was new to the battlefield and held positions at various locations beyond the Siegfried Line, for example the 3rd Battalion of the 393rd Infantry in Hollerath. When the 277th Volksgrenadier Division moved forward, much of the battalion was swallowed up and compelled to surrender or fall back. Two of the platoons in Company K lost all personnel as casualties or prisoners. The remaining platoon had a better defensive position and for a time inflicted punishing losses on the enemy infantry. However, those members of the 3rd Battalion who could do so retired with most of their wounded along a forest trail to re-form behind a line held by the 3rd Battalion, 23rd Infantry of the 2nd Division, with the intention of extending the left flank of that line.[4]

The 2nd Division fought in Normandy and was an established regular army unit consisting of 9th, 23rd and 38th Infantry Regiments with the normal divisional artillery battalions and support elements. The division was positioned for an offensive to the north at the Wahlerscheid crossroads. A portion of the 23rd Infantry – the 3rd Battalion – established a line along the woods trail on the evening of 16 December and supplemented the defences maintained by the 393rd Infantry. However, the overall defences stood in the path of advancing tanks and young infantry from the 12th SS Panzer Division. Company I of the 23rd commanded by Captain Charles MacDonald, later an army historian and author of *A Time for Trumpets* among other books, held against repeated attacks, but the end was near. Armoured forces overran the company, and its 1st Platoon was essentially destroyed. The other companies in the battalion line eventually also unravelled. One soldier – Private First Class José Lopez – was so stalwart in defence he received the Medal of Honor.[5] The 393rd Infantry later complained their line was undermined by the collapse.[6]

Another battalion formed a line along the trail, the 1/9th Infantry under Lieutenant Colonel William McKinley. The ultimate purpose of all these defensive positions was to protect a road leading south from Wahlerscheid to the 'twin' villages of Rocherath and Krinkelt and the road west through Wirtzfeld leading to the Elsenborn Ridge. As the magnitude of the offensive developed, it became clear the 2nd and 99th Division units must withdraw southward along a line perpendicular to that of the German advance westward. McKinley's battalion supplemented by portions of another company held for hours. On the evening of 17 December messages received indicated tanks had broken through the position held by 1/9th and were heading for Rocherath.[7] Early on the morning of 18 December McKinley reported, 'We have been strenuously engaged. Have knocked out three tiger tanks. Others have infiltrated my position. Have situation in hand at present.' A slightly later message from another source indicated 'Krinkelt and Rocherath are full of Krauts.'[8] (Reports of 'tiger tanks' near the twin villages were common but inaccurate. MacDonald later thought they may reflect the presence of *Jagdpanther* armoured anti-tank vehicles mounting the same 88mm gun as Tiger tanks.[9])

McKinley's battalion eventually withdrew about midday on the 18th but not before troops moving southward passed through the crossroads behind the battalion position. The 38th report rather tersely noted their movement was 'covered to some extent' by the 1/9th Infantry holding the road junction east of Rocherath, but their commander Colonel Francis Boos was closer to the mark in telling McKinley the battalion stand saved his regiment. McKinley's forces paid a high price: the 1/9th and the additional Company K collectively numbered around 600 soldiers but only slightly more than 200 were present after the withdrawal. MacDonald thought it was the most significant of all the early efforts on the northern edge and among the most stalwart of any by American troops in the Ardennes.[10]

The ensuing battles in the twin villages of Rocherath and Krinkelt were disorganized, confused and deadly. German troops entered from the east as the small armoured force of three Panzerjägers (tank destroyers) with Obersturmführer Zeiner that pushed through McKinley's position occupied the northern part of Rocherath. They destroyed some American armour and held for most of the night, withdrawing with prisoners early on the 18th.[11]

A larger German force was advancing on the villages that morning, resulting in confused close-quarter fighting on the 18th. The contest re-emphasized problems encountered by and vulnerability of tanks in the narrow streets of villages and towns, where superiority of guns and thickness of armour mattered little at short ranges. Scattered remnants of American units held tenaciously in stone-walled houses and stalked German tanks through streets and alleys. During the afternoon the commanding officer of Company K reported nearly all contact with his company had been lost while the commander of the 3/23rd Infantry – Lieutenant Colonel Paul Tuttle – held out in Krinkelt with 'odds and ends'. Tensions were reflected in relationships between infantry and armour. The 2nd Battalion of the 23rd was supported by three tanks. During the morning one was 'knocked over' and another moved back. The commander of the third tank was informed that 'if he moved the G Co 23d would shoot them with a bazooka'.[12]

The attack on the twin villages by Panthers from 1 and 3 Companies of the division's panzer regiment resulted in a cemetery for the German tanks with vehicles destroyed in the centre of the villages near the church and along the central road. The 3 Company leader, Brödel, was dead in the turret of his destroyed Panther while platoon leader Beutelhauser managed to escape from his tank. The tank of Willi Fischer in the same platoon lost a track when struck by an anti-tank gun or tank destroyer shell. The villages contained mixtures of American soldiers who opposed German infantry and fired on crewmen who survived destruction of their tanks. Another platoon leader in 3 Company, Willi Engel, observed a Panther in the centre of the villages burst into flames, having been struck by an immobile Sherman that could still fire its gun.[13]

Many structures in the villages were reduced to rubble when American forces decided to pull the defenders back on the night of 18-19 December to stronger positions on Elsenborn Ridge. Had the Germans (12th SS and 277th Divisions initially) not attempted to pass through the twin villages but circled to the south then approached Elsenborn Ridge moving north-east through Bütgenbach early on the 17 December, their chances of success may have been greater. Perhaps more feasibly, if Kampfgruppe Peiper upon reaching Büllingen on the 17th had moved that way in force it would very likely have progressed further, thereby enabling 12th SS and associated forces to move in concert.

Yet as early as 7.00am elements of the US 1st Infantry Division – the 3rd Battalion of the 26th Infantry – arrived at Elsenborn and by early afternoon occupied Bütgenbach. The 2nd Battalion led by Lieutenant Colonel Derrill Daniel assumed positions on and behind a crest occupied by estate buildings of Domaine Bütgenbach on the road leading east to Büllingen.[14]

Relatively little happened on the 18th although fighting in the twin villages was clearly evident and troops were moving from the villages to positions near Elsenborn.

In addition, columns from the 1st SS Panzer Division continued moving through Büllingen. On the 19th things began to heat up as the 12th SS Panzers initiated attacks over more than three days with the aim of breaking through to Elsenborn. Early in the morning, armour and some twenty truckloads of infantry advanced in front of Company E. Artillery knocked out three tanks and dispersed the infantry. Companies from 1st Battalion occupied high ground about 1,000 yards south of Bütgenbach astride the road leading to 2nd Battalion positions. Later in the morning, a tank was stopped by an anti-tank gun that was in turn destroyed; as stated later, 'Had two men killed in action, one blinded and other nerves shot. They knocked out a tank and recon vehicle.' On this day crews manning 57mm guns used British 6-pounder discarding sabot ammunition, thereby increasing the velocity of shells fired from the normally ineffective piece.[15]

Artillery fire fell on Company E positions in the early morning darkness of 20 December and appeared to be quelled by counter-battery responses from the 33rd Field Artillery Battalion. This situation however proved to be a calm before the storm as roughly twenty tanks and a battalion of Panzergrenadiers advanced around 3.30am. American artillery support again rose to the occasion but German cannon and mortars pounded the US lines. German tanks broke through between Companies E and F but the infantry continued to resist the 'most intense pressure ever experienced' by those companies from advancing Panzergrenadiers. Five tanks pulled up about 100 yards from the battalion command post at the domaine and opened fire. Anti-tank guns wrote off two tanks and the remainder withdrew a distance. A lull in the action occurred about 5.30am but artillery fire continued to fall on the lines. The Germans sought to exploit or renew their breakthrough between the two companies throughout the day but were stymied by continued American artillery support.[16]

The following day – 21 December – began with a heavy artillery barrage on the American lines followed at 4.00am by another major German effort to force a breakthrough. These attacks were elements of a larger plan to circle behind Domaine Bütgenbach and reduce the position from eastern and western directions as other troops advanced on Elsenborn to overrun the devastating concentration of American artillery. The attacks were conducted by troops from 12th Volksgrenadier and the 12th SS Panzer Divisions. The latter included infantry from Panzergrenadier Regiment 26, with a battalion from the 25th, supported by heavy *Jagdpanther* vehicles, surviving Panther tanks from 3 Company and Mark IV tanks from 5 Company.[17]

Six tanks were destroyed by artillery fire and burned in front of the lines but five others broke through the Company G position. These intruders moved into shelter among the buildings on the domaine property. The battalion called for mortar fire that compelled the tanks to seek new positions, but movement exposed them to anti-tank guns. By 4.00pm all five were out of action; as the regimental report recounted, the tank destroyers and anti-tank crews either destroyed the enemy or were themselves eliminated.

The infantry lines with ample artillery support held against repeated attacks. Lieutenant Colonel Daniel was unreserved in his praise during the afternoon: 'The artillery did a great job, I don't know where they got the ammo or when they took time to flush the guns but we wouldn't be here if it wasn't for them. There were 100 of them that came at one plat[oon] and not one of them got thru.'[18]

Efforts resumed on 22 December against the 26th Infantry's 1st and 3rd Battalions. The position on the left of Company A was struck at 6.30am by six tanks and several hundred infantry soldiers. Company B moved south from Bütgenbach through Company A then pivoted east against the Germans. The fighting continued throughout the morning; the line stabilized by mid-afternoon. An attack largely or exclusively by armour was resisted by Company K.[19] The line held as Lieutenant Colonel Daniel said it would.

Kampfgruppe Peiper

The spearhead for the 1st SS Panzer Division assault south of the 12th SS was headed by Obersturmbannführer (Lieutenant Colonel) Joachim Peiper, a trusted soldier in the division who emerged from previous service with a reputation for bold and ruthless actions. The advance of certain units under his command would be characterized by both behaviours during the first days in the Ardennes.

Kampfgruppe Peiper was a substantial motorized force that included most of the division's Mark IV and Panther tanks, assault guns and Panzerjägers, self-propelled 20mm anti-aircraft guns, a battalion of Panzergrenadier infantry in armoured personnel carriers, reconnaissance and engineer troops and in the rear – due to their weight and cumbersome nature – Tiger B tanks in a heavy panzer battalion. These formidable vehicles would exploit the expected breakthrough. As it developed they became embroiled in fighting both in Stavelot and later at La Gleize.

After some initial delays, the column that stretched back for miles began moving with purpose on the 17th. American positions were overrun at Losheimergraben on the frontier and then at Honsfeld where numerous soldiers were shot following surrender. The lead portion of the column moved northward to Büllingen to refuel from seized petrol supplies. Although at least one wounded prisoner was shot, the numerous killings were not repeated. A small group of tanks and infantry probed up the northern road, crossing a ridge south of Wirtzfeld. An improvised US force including self-propelled tank destroyers fired on and damaged several vehicles, causing the others to retire to Büllingen.[20]

Peiper at the head of the column sought to move quickly and so turned south-west in the general direction of Saint-Vith but soon resumed a westward course past Malmédy, a place likely to be defended and thus to be avoided. At a crossroads called

Baunez a few miles south of Malmédy, advance elements collided with trucks carrying an American support unit, Battery B, 285th Field Artillery Observation Battalion that was heading south. Certainly no match for an armoured column that shot up most of the vehicles, more than one hundred soldiers including some from other units quickly became prisoners.

Peiper came upon the scene and restored order to the impromptu conflict. After interrogating a prisoner and lamenting the unnecessary destruction of trucks, he continued with the vanguard south to Ligneuville. Sometime after he departed an SS officer in the kampfgruppe ordered two tanks to train their guns on the rows of prisoners in a field. Machine gun and pistol fire tore into the packed mass. Later some engineer troops moved through the field, shooting anyone who appeared to remain alive. Some retreated into a café but were driven out and shot when the building was set ablaze.

Despite the apparent thoroughness of these murders, survivors remained in the field, in a shed or even in the burning ruins of the café to bear witness to the atrocity. Eventually they would make their way in small groups to Malmédy with the assistance of Belgian civilians or US troops who drove uphill to the crossroads from the town. Forty-three soldiers survived, wounded or not, but eighty-six (in addition to civilians) lost their lives.

Once survivors reached Malmédy word spread quickly. An intelligence report provided the testimony of one who survived and further repeated the evaluation of the 1st Division intelligence officer that the responsible unit was thought to be 1st SS Reconnaissance Battalion. Other atrocities were attributed to this unit en route to Stavelot at the village of Parfondruy, specifically the murder of twenty-six civilians including at least two women. Nearby in Renardmont civilians were reported shot in their homes. A woman who spoke German and her two children were spared but twenty-three others in her group, all but two women and children, were shot in Stavelot. One resident swam the River Amblève in Trois-Ponts to escape; others from his group were later killed. An elderly couple was shot down along a road in the same village.[21]

American reactions were swift. Following widespread distribution of information on events near Malmédy – no doubt at times embellished but the truth was awful enough – many were filled with hatred and at least one unit refused to accept any German surrenders for more than a week. A similar anger grew within 3rd Armoured Division when evidence of the labour camps at Mittlebau-Dora was revealed in April 1945.[22]

Peiper continued to Ligneuville where a brief fight delayed the column. On the move again, they proceeded along the south side of the River Amblève along a winding road towards Stavelot and its stone bridge. Delayed by a small detachment and seeing many headlights across the valley in Stavelot, he decided to give his troops rest before proceeding early on the 18th.

The passage next morning across the river and through the town was accomplished fairly quickly despite losing some tanks to a few American anti-tank guns. The column headed west on the morning of the 18th to Trois-Ponts seeking bridges carrying roads to Werbomont and beyond to the Meuse. An act of self-sacrifice by a 57mm crew of four not only disabled one lead Panther but alerted the 51st Engineers to blow two bridges in town, while the third south of town was destroyed later. Peiper could only head north along the Amblève to La Gleize where the 30th Division would oppose them at Stoumont while the 504th Parachute Infantry would recapture Cheneux and its nearby bridge. Kampfgruppe Peiper would be hemmed in by these opponents.[23]

Bastogne

The town of Bastogne – an important road junction in the centre of what emerged as the German 'Bulge' – lay in the path of the central advance by Fifth Panzer Army. The 101st Airborne Division departed for the town with little advance notice and arrived on 19 December. Armoured units formed teams to defend positions east and north of the town. The defenders were soon isolated as German forces moved past heading for the Meuse. Tank destroyer units and tank elements derived from two armoured divisions (9th and 10th), while still small in comparison to the forces that bedeviled the garrison, provided essential support in Bastogne.

The defenders of Bastogne endured shortages of supplies, bombing raids that killed or wounded soldiers and civilians, and attempts to overrun the town. Frustrated by their lack of success in compelling the defenders to surrender, a concerted effort was launched by the Germans from the north-west to break through defences. One attack fell upon a battalion from the 502nd Parachute Infantry centred on the village of Champs on a road to Bastogne. The second location was an adjoining area between Champs and the Marche to Bastogne highway held by 3rd Battalion of the 327th Glider Infantry. The determined effort would be staged by infantry from the 26th Volksgrenadier Division, an infantry regiment from the 15th Panzergrenadier Division, some self-propelled artillery and eighteen Mark IV and Panther tanks.

The initial attack was launched early on Christmas morning by the Volksgrenadiers against a company from the 1/502nd in Champs. The battalion commander, Major John Hanlon, was reluctant to send his other companies into the pre-dawn confusion in the village, choosing instead to occupy high ground nearby to provide a potential haven should those in Champs need to retire. The Panzergrenadiers and tanks penetrated forward positions of the 327th and headed for Hemroulle on the road leading from Champs to Bastogne. The armoured column split with a portion turning to circle behind Champs while the other section continued on to Hemroulle and it was hoped Bastogne. The reconnaissance battalion of the 26th Volksgrenadier Division would also participate by seeking a way from Senonchamps north to the Marche–Bastogne highway.

The portion heading for the rear of Champs confronted the two companies from 1/502nd that fell back to a wooded area. Their gunfire concentrated on the exposed infantry riding on the tanks while bazookas and attached tank destroyers claimed five of the tanks. The other section moving to Hemroulle was caught in fire from tanks and tank destroyers in addition to artillery and bazookas with the glider infantry. The soldiers from the 1/115th Volksgrenadier Regiment on the tanks were again either killed or left without support as the tanks were disabled. The 2/115th moved further but was observed at daybreak and subjected to fire from a 327th Glider Infantry company supported by artillery and mortars.

German infantry in Champs left the fighting in the village during the morning to continue an uphill assault to Hemroulle but these troops were also stopped. A final effort originating from south of the Marche–Bastogne highway early on 26 December by Volksgrenadiers and some Panzerjägers met with the same fate.[24]

The airborne troops and their attached units held the town and surrounding countryside through Christmas until forces from Third Army reached the southern perimeter late on 26 December. More than 700 wounded in the town suffered from inadequate care due a lack of supplies and limited personnel. The 326th Airborne Medical Company had been overrun west of Bastogne shortly after the division arrived. Medical tents and trucks were fired upon and the divisional surgeon, Lieutenant Colonel David Gold, surrendered the facility. Surgical teams and supplies were desperately needed and some were transported into the perimeter by gliders, one of which landed near the German lines. 'The medical personnel barreled out, ran back to our lines and the doughboys attacked in the vicinity of the glider then under fire by German machine guns, rescued the craft and the medical supplies it carried.'[25]

Third Army Response

The meeting in Verdun on 19 December was called to organize the American defence in response to the offensive. Once Patton had been informed by Omar Bradley of the overall gravity of the situation and the necessity to transfer one armoured division northward immediately, the planned offensive for Third Army into the Saar region was called off. Before leaving for the Verdun meeting he devised a plan for an advance along three axes northward into the southern flank of the German advance and would inform his staff following the meeting using a simple code which axis would be emphasized.

The situation on 19 December as later summarized by Third Army appeared grim. The 106th Division had lost two regiments. The third regiment and 7th Armoured Division were also thought to be to the north, but in fact were fighting to support those troops holding onto Saint-Vith. The 101st Airborne would soon be surrounded in Bastogne with one combat command each from 9th and 10th Armoured. The 28th Division was split into separate elements with the 109th Infantry attached to another 9th Armoured combat command in the southern portion of the salient. The 9th Armoured was divided into three parts: one in the north, one in Bastogne and the third Combat Command A in the south with 109th Infantry.[26]

Most of Third Army would reorient and move northward over the next few days, with III Corps among others advancing on the important road junction of Bastogne. When Patton announced he hoped to launch an attack within two days, many in the room including Eisenhower frankly believed that to be impossible. Ike stated he wanted any response to be a strong one and urged Patton not to attack before sufficient forces were assembled. The effort by III Corps (4th Armoured, 26th and 80th Infantry Divisions) jumped off from Arlon west of Luxembourg on the morning of the 22nd. Given the immense logistical challenges associated with reorienting tens of thousands of troops and vehicles and advancing roughly 75 miles to attack in a different direction, Bradley gained an enhanced respect for Patton and the staff of Third Army.[27]

Progress was fairly rapid initially and the next day the overcast and snowy weather moderated and clear skies emerged. Patton attributed the improvement to a 'weather prayer' he asked the Third Army chaplain to write. Movement towards Bastogne continued but Third Army was unable to reach the defensive perimeter by Christmas Day in the face of stiffened resistance. Patton noted with pride that many men received a hot Christmas dinner and those in direct contact with the enemy at least had chicken sandwiches.[28]

Elements of the 4th Armoured Division from Third Army finally made contact with the southern edge of the Bastogne perimeter on the late afternoon and evening of 26 December. A narrow corridor was opened enabling supplies to enter and the first ambulances to evacuate the more seriously wounded. Casualty removals were completed on the 27th. Hansen commented: 'Youngsters who had lost an arm or leg and had been lying for five or six days in many cases without surgical treatment, forgot their own wounds, forgot the loss of arms and legs, forgot the misery and the suffering that surrounded them and could talk of nothing but the reply of their general [McAuliffe who responded 'Nuts'] to the German commander.'[29]

Other memories of Christmas 1944 exist. Peter Munger was an enlisted soldier with the 120th Infantry in the 30th Division. He remembered passing a field on patrol only to learn later it was the scene of the Malmédy massacre. The bodies were covered in snow when the patrol moved past. During that or another patrol they could tell Germans previously occupied a wooded area due to the smell probably from their soap. (A sense of smell was important on the front line but is rarely mentioned. The men had become hunters with acute senses as keys to survival.) Finally, he recalled his commander procured a Christmas orange for each man in the company, which he still thought was marvellous. Soldiers in the regiment received a Christmas stocking: a winter wool sock with candy and the other sock from the pair inside. However, many donated their stockings to children in Malmédy injured in repeated mistaken bombings of the town. As had been the case in late July in Normandy, the 30th Division again became the targets of the American Air Corps. Citizens of a Belgian town that had been shielded from German reoccupation were victims of the same bombings.[30]

Reactions

Chet Hansen, an aide to Bradley, recorded command reactions to the events early in the offensive. He travelled to Verdun and while not a participant provided impressions both before and following the meeting, in addition to summarizing major decisions.[31] Upon leaving Luxembourg they were keenly aware of anxiety among the citizens in a city being flooded by refugees from towns to the north and east. Residents feared the return of the Germans and their expected reprisals for assistance provided to the Allies since September. However, so much American military traffic was moving into the city Hansen believed the citizenry would take heart. In any event, Bradley was determined to retain control of Luxembourg. Actually, he later stated the meeting was held primarily to arrange a shift in responsibility for the Saar front to the 6th Army Group, since Eisenhower had already approved the movement of Third Army northward to strike the expanding German salient.[32]

Hansen's diary provided a wealth of information relating to personalities and decisions during the campaign in north-west Europe. The entries were particularly illuminating in the period of the Ardennes offensive. On 20 December he summarized the impact to date:

When the weight of the German offensive rolled back through our lines he found no depth since our skin was stretched at this juncture to allow strength for the First, Ninth and Third Army offensives into the Siegfried Line. Disorganization has resulted in the rear areas with some moderate loss of traffic control and the free movements of enemy spearheads has given rise to many unfounded rumors of his advances.

Bradley and other American officers decried the overcast weather that prevented air support at which the Allies excelled. As Hansen stated: 'with two good days in the air, we could decimate his supply lines, arrest road movement and knock out his troop carrying transports.' By 23 December the skies had cleared and air assaults on German columns and aerial resupply of surrounded troops could begin.

As a result of the breakthrough and resulting communication difficulties, Bernard Montgomery gained control of American forces on the northern side of the salient – essentially all of First Army. Bradley hoped to amass a reserve force of sufficient strength to strike back immediately once the German advance had been contained.

On the 24th Hansen complained Monty was employing regiments piecemeal and thus dissipating the potential reserve. While this comment was strictly true at that point, Courtney Hodges in command of First Army found it necessary to use the reserve Montgomery wished to preserve.

On New Year's Eve in Luxembourg, a small gathering that included the journalist Martha Gelhorn assembled at General Bradley's headquarters to ring in the new year. Another journalist, Bill Walton, suggested the world had never been 'plagued by such a year less worth remembering' than 1944.[33] Others – in France and western Belgium – who suffered through four years of German occupation would regard the summer and fall of 1944 as a time of liberation. Troops in the field would spend a cold and often cheerless evening before the advent of 1945.

Dock workers loading artillery shells on a munitions ship in Charleston, South Carolina in December 1944. *(NARA)*

Infantry bound for Europe moving off a ferry towards a transport ship in New York harbor in December. The need for replacements and new infantry units would soon expand at an alarming rate and such units would not look as clean and crisp after a few weeks in the field. (NARA)

The 121st Infantry in the 9th Division moved through the shattered town of Hürtgen on 30 November. (NARA)

(**Opposite, above**) Two soldiers seeking shelter beside a Sherman in Geich, Germany, on 11 December. (*NARA*)

(**Opposite, below**) Allen photographed a 28th Division soldier performing the role of Father Christmas, or Saint Nickolas, for a local pageant in Wiltz, Luxembourg, on 5 December. One of the local girls in the jeep remembered the day with great fondness when interviewed by Tom Lemmon for the 1994 documentary film *The Battle of the Bulge*. (*NARA*)

(**Above**) American troops riding on a captured Tiger B tank painted with a white star in Gersonsweiller, Germany, as photographed by Sanderson on 15 December. (*NARA*)

(**Opposite, above**) The town of Düren on the River Roer was an objective of American troops in November. Hidden dangers lurked in the streets even after occupation. The driver of a Sherman did not see a water-filled shell hole at night. Roberts witnessed the scene on 15 December. (*NARA*)

(**Opposite, below**) The 399th Infantry in the 100th Division occupied a shallow zig-zag trench in the woods near Bitche, France, on 18 December. They probably did not realize a German offensive had been unleashed to the north in the Ardennes two days earlier. (*NARA*)

(**Above**) A German propaganda film unit travelled with the assault troops to provide a morale boost for soldiers and civilians in the Reich. Still frames from a captured copy of the film yielded interesting images of soldiers from the 1st SS Panzer Division apparently on 17 December. A soldier waved for comrades to follow during the advance. (*NARA*)

A Tiger B or *Königstiger* tank from a heavy panzer battalion possibly attached to Kampfgruppe Peiper passed a line of American prisoners in the early days of the offensive. (*NARA*)

German soldiers running across a road with abandoned American equipment in the background. (*NARA*)

Soldiers move forward past an armoured vehicle, possibly an American light tank. Snow has not fallen in portions of the Ardennes at this point. (*NARA*)

A group of soldiers with cigarettes likely obtained from American supplies. One member of the group appears in the next photograph. (*NARA*)

The haggard face of this same soldier has been used frequently to convey the rigours of war during the winter campaign. He carried machine gun ammunition over his shoulders. *(NARA)*

Soldiers passing an American half-track or personnel carrier emblazoned with a white star. The propaganda value of such a photograph was unmistakable. (*NARA*)

(**Opposite, above**) The crew of a Jagdpanzer IV or armoured anti-tank vehicle moving forward. Based on a Mark IV tank chassis, this model appears to mount the long-barrelled 75mm gun that proved effective against American Sherman tanks. The vehicle was less successful when, due to dwindling quantities of German armour late in the war, it was employed as an assault gun. (*NARA*)

(**Above**) Soldiers advance past burning American vehicles. (*NARA*)

(**Opposite, below**) Soldiers, probably officers, walking along a road near a signpost. The respective distances to Malmédy and Saint-Vith indicate the location was likely a junction of roads leading south from Waimes and Büllingen to Saint-Vith, or another road south from Malmédy at an intersection with a sideroad to Recht. These junctions lay in the path of the 2nd SS Panzer Grenadier Regiment from the 1st SS Panzer Division. The regiment advanced on a parallel line south of Kampfgruppe Peiper. (*NARA*)

German officer reading a map adjacent to the road sign. (*NARA*)

Two SS officers conferring during the early days of the Ardennes offensive. One seemed displeased at the prospect of being photographed. (*NARA*)

Americans captured in one of the villages, possibly Honsfeld, near the front during the early days of the Ardennes offensive. (NARA)

American casualties sprawled near 3-inch anti-tank guns overrun early in the offensive. Anti-tank guns were present in Honsfeld. Some US soldiers were killed while a number of prisoners were shot in the town. (NARA)

(**Above**) These American soldiers may have been among the first prisoners to be shot during the offensive. The signpost denotes directions to Büllingen 5km away and a rail station. Another photograph revealed the post pointed to Losheimergraben 4km in the opposite direction from Büllingen. The town is thus revealed to be Honsfeld between the two locations. The boots have been removed from one American body and a German soldier standing near the signpost may be trying them on for size. (*NARA*)

(**Opposite**) A small German force from 1st SS Panzer Division moved north from Büllingen on 17 December en route to Wirtzfeld and a junction with 12th SS troops expected to be in the area. The movement was observed by the 644th Tank Destroyer Battalion south-east of Wirtzfeld that opened fire and stopped the tanks and personnel carriers (MacDonald, *Time for Trumpets,* 210; Cavanagh, *Battle East of Elsenborn,* 69–70). Zaloga attributed this Panther 126 to an attack by 12th SS Panzer on the morning of 18 December. The tank managed to escape the mêlée in Krinkelt after sustaining several strikes from bazooka rockets and anti-tank guns. One of the 644th tank destroyers fired into the more vulnerable rear of the vehicle, setting it ablaze (*Smashing Hitler's Panzers,* 232–4). Panther 126 – denoting tank No. 6 in the second *Zug* or platoon in the first company – was still burning in these photographs by Clancy dated 17 December but evidently recorded later. A crew member was being escorted by Sergeant Bernard Cook of Los Angeles. (*NARA*)

(**Above**) The Americans began to capture Germans early in the offensive. This young paratrooper with an injured cheek was probably a member of the von der Heydte unit and may have been injured during his jump. Petrony recorded the image on 17 December. *(NARA)*

(**Opposite, above**) Another destroyed tank – probably a Mark IV – on the road to Wirtzfeld in a photograph also dated 17 December. Clancy observed Private First Class William Boyd and Sergeant Jesse Velasquez on the ruined vehicle *(NARA)*

(**Opposite, below**) The battle in the villages of Krinkelt and Rocherath to the north provided a clear example of the dangers posed to armoured vehicles even in smaller towns and villages. This badly damaged Panther was a casualty of the ferocious close quarter fighting when 1 and 3 Companies attacked on 18 December. This vehicle – probably No. 318 denoting the eighth tank in the first platoon of 3 Company – burned, sustained damage to its right track, and most dramatically lost its gun barrel in front of the Kalpers home on the street in Rocherath (Campbell, *East of Elsenborn*, 171–2; Zaloga, *Smashing Hitler's Panzers*; www.miaproject.net). The photograph was attributed to Clancy on 17 December but the date seems incorrect. *(NARA)*

(**Above**) A member of 2nd Engineer Battalion planting mines along the edge of the road near Wirtzfeld on 18 December. (*NARA*)

(**Opposite, above**) Members of 26th Infantry moving up to Domaine Bütgenbach on 17 December as seen by Bellere. By late afternoon and early evening that day the regiment established a strong defensive position at the domaine estate and nearby town. (*NARA*)

(**Opposite, below**) A tank destroyer at Dom. Bütgenbach that defended the line held by 2nd Battalion of 26th Infantry. An abandoned German tank was visible just beyond the position. Photo by Augustine undated but possibly 22 December. (*NARA*)

199680

(**Opposite, above**) Shub visited the road leading to Bütgenbach on 1 February 1945 and found the verges covered with destroyed and abandoned German armour. (*NARA*)

(**Opposite, below**) A view of the landscape in 2001 facing north-west to the twin villages of Krinkelt and Rocherath.

(**Above**) Portion of a massive American gasoline depot on 7 December 1944 near Spa in Belgium. Seizure of gasoline was required to maintain the offensive but the Germans were unaware of the precise locations of these depots. An attempt to capture one near Stavelot was thwarted by a small group of soldiers who erected a flaming barrier of burning 'Jerricans' filled with gasoline. (*NARA*)

(**Above**) The burned ruins of a portion of an American fuel dump near Stavelot on 19 December, the results of the flaming barrier. (*NARA*)

(**Opposite, above**) View of Stavelot facing south-west in late December. The town and its small stone bridge over the River Amblève assumed considerable importance. Kampfgruppe Peiper crossed the bridge from the south early on the 18th and moved along the river to Trois-Ponts where bridges were blown up just in front of them. The column then turned northward to La Gleize in an increasingly desperate effort to reach the Meuse.

American soldiers from the 117th Infantry with supporting artillery reoccupied much of Stavelot on the 18th. Elements of the 2nd SS Panzergrenadier Regiment with four Panther tanks attacked in an effort to reopen the supply line to Peiper later that day and on the 19th. They sought to cross the stone bridge but were unsuccessful. The reconnaissance battalion from the 1st SS Panzer Division under Major Gustav Knittel passed through with Obersturmbannführer Joachim Peiper on the 18th but returned to attack from the west without success on the 19th. The bridge was finally destroyed (or damaged) by American engineers later on the evening of the 19th. Still, elements of 2nd SS Panzer Regiment attempted to cross on the 20th but were again driven back to the south bank (MacDonald, *Time for Trumpets*, 434–7).

Despite the apparent demolition, the bridge appeared reasonably intact in this photograph dated 30 December. Damage in the town and debris from the battles were evident. In addition to the German Tiger B tank visible on the south bank, other vehicles were evidently abandoned on the bridge and an armoured vehicle or possibly US anti-tank gun was present at the north end. (*NARA*)

(**Opposite, below**) A dead German soldier on Stavelot street photographed on 21 December. (*NARA*)

Members of the 117th Infantry from the 30th Division prepare to enter a house sheltering snipers in Stavelot on 21 December. (*NARA*)

Calvano recorded three soldiers from the 2nd Battalion 120th Infantry (Peter Munger belonged to that battalion) manning a machine-gun post probably south of Malmédy on 21 December. No snow had fallen in the area by that date. (*NARA*)

On 22 December McHugh encountered groups of civilians murdered in Stavelot during the brief German occupation. The killing of residents began in the town as Kampfgruppe Peiper passed through early on the 18th. The victims had been shot or bore traces of rifle butt injuries. More than one hundred cases of civilian murder or disappearances were documented in villages and houses along the route of advance by Peiper's troops (MacDonald, *Time for Trumpets*, 437–8). (*NARA*)

The burial of civilians in Stavelot on 30 December. (*NARA*)

Several vehicles from the heavy panzer battalion attached to Kampfgruppe Peiper were disabled on narrow streets during an attempt to drive the Americans from the town. Soldiers peered at one of those Tiger B tanks on 21 December as photographed by Calvano. (*NARA*)

(**Above**) Calvano photographed a church amid the ruins of Stavelot on 21 December. (*NARA*)

(**Opposite, above**) Bodies of American soldiers from a field artillery observation unit were found beneath the snow in fields around the Baunez crossroads south of Malmédy. The soldiers were shot shortly after surrendering on 17 December during the advance of Kampfgruppe Peiper. Burned ruins of crossroads buildings remained visible. (*NARA*)

(**Opposite, below**) Investigations of more than eighty American bodies covered in snow were undertaken in January 1945. Taylor photographed two African American stretcher bearers carrying one soldier from the field on 16 January. (*NARA*)

(**Opposite, above**) A soldier left unburied beneath the snow with burned buildings at the crossroads in the background. (*NARA*)

(**Opposite, below**) A cluster of victims near the Baunez crossroads. Investigators placed numbers next to bodies to aid identification and assist in reconstructing the terrible events that unfolded on 17 December. Members of the 1st SS Panzer Division including Peiper were later charged with the murders of unarmed prisoners. (*NARA*)

(**Above**) Henri Lejoly was a local resident who witnessed the murders at Baunez. Before the shooting he directed Germans to a shed where some Americans sought shelter. Madame Bodarwé owned a crossroads café north of the field into which the prisoners had been gathered. Once the Germans saw soldiers running into the café, they set fire to the building and shot those who emerged. Lejoly survived to be photographed by Taylor on 16 January but Madame Bodarwé disappeared without a trace (MacDonald, *Time for Trumpets*, 217–8, 221–2). (*NARA*)

(**Opposite, above**) Aerial view of village near Bastogne with vehicles and tracks in snow-covered fields on 3 January 1945. (*NARA*)

(**Opposite, below**) Bonwitt photographed a 3-inch anti-tank gun unit from 7th Armoured Division positioned on a road near Vielsalm on 23 December. (*NARA*)

(**Above**) Lieutenant Colonel James LaPrade assumed command of the 1/506th Parachute Infantry in Normandy following the death of the previous battalion leader. LaPrade was killed by an artillery shell-burst during the defence of Noville north of Bastogne on 19 December. Krochka recorded an image of his grave on 28 December. (*NARA*)

A scene of the countryside near Bastogne in late December with supply planes flying at low altitudes overhead. (NARA)

Planes took advantage of clear weather to fly supply missions over and near Bastogne on Christmas Day. Krochka recorded this present for the 101st Airborne. (NARA)

A military policeman watches 23rd Tank Battalion of 12th Armoured Division pass on 26 December, as photographed by Howell. (*NARA*)

Carol recorded an image of two soldiers in the town of Bastogne probably in December. (*NARA*)

198651-S

(**Above**) Krochka stood on a street in Bastogne on 26 December as buildings appeared to be burning and one citizen was running. While artillery may have been falling, other residents on the street appeared unconcerned. (*NARA*)

(**Opposite, above**) Soldiers from the 10th Infantry Battalion of the 4th Armoured Division moved northward across open fields to Bastogne on 27 December. Tanks from the division entered the defensive perimeter south of town the previous evening. (*NARA*)

(**Opposite, below**) Two riflemen from the 10th Infantry Battalion provide covering fire as the infantry battalion advances with 4th Armoured Division on the 27th. (*NARA*)

(**Opposite, above**) 101st soldiers dragged bundles from an aerial resupply mission on the 27th. The photographer Krochka captured the image. (*NARA*)

(**Opposite, below**) Gilbert recorded an image of German prisoners of the 4th Armoured Division near Bastogne in late December. (*NARA*)

(**Above**) Patients in Bastogne who would shortly be evacuated to more adequate hospital facilities, as photographed by Krochka on 27 December. (*NARA*)

(**Opposite, above**) One of the Mark IV panzers stopped by defenders while trying to enter Bastogne from the west on Christmas Day. Krochka recorded this superb image of the tank on 26 December. (*NARA*)

(**Opposite, below**) Generals Maxwell Taylor (at left) and Anthony McAuliffe of the 101st Airborne Division in Bastogne on 5 January photographed by Sullivan. Since Taylor was attending War Department meetings in Washington when the offensive began, McAuliffe commanded the division during movement to and occupation of Bastogne and offered the famous 'Nuts' refusal to the German surrender demand. Helmet stencils and short tic marks used in the division are clearly visible: a circular cannonball since McAuliffe was the designated commander of divisional artillery and a square denoting division headquarters. (*NARA*)

(**Above**) Carolan observed members of the 101st marching north along 'the road to Houffalize' on 29 December. (*NARA*)

(**Above**) These 101st soldiers returning from a night patrol were planning to secure breakfast from ration cartons on 31 December. (*NARA*)

(**Opposite, above**) A group from the 101st prepared to advance near Bastogne on the same day, 31 December, as photographed by Gilbert. (*NARA*)

(**Opposite, below**) Ornitz recorded an image of 35th Tank Battalion from the 4th Armoured Division advancing on Sainlez south of Bastogne on the 31st. (*NARA*)

Civilians in Sainlez gather remaining grain from the ruins of a barn or granary on 28 December. (*NARA*)

Chapter Two

The Ardennes Winter

Fifth Panzer Army in the centre advanced well beyond the American lines and in doing so eliminated much of two American divisions. The 106th Division only moved to the front line in the Schnee Eifel east of Saint-Vith about one week before the attack. The forward two regiments became isolated by a double envelopment movement north and south of their positions. They attempted to attack westward to break out of the encirclement, anticipating that forces outside – first from 9th Armoured then a planned assault from 7th Armoured Division – would force an opening, thereby taking a page from German escapes from pockets on the Eastern Front and in Normandy. Pressure beyond the pocket was never exerted and the two regiments advanced without strong mutual coordination but could not break through the enemy forces near Schönberg. Facing annihilation, the encircled units surrendered on 19 December. The 106th Division was reduced to only one infantry regiment and supporting troops.[1]

Once the 106th Division troops in the Schnee Eifel were forced to surrender, advancing German divisions in Fifth Panzer Army turned their attention to Saint-Vith. A defensive line of sorts was formed just east of the town from a patchwork of units in the vicinity. Two combat commands from 7th Armoured Division and one from 9th Armoured Division covered areas from Poteau in the north-west forward to and then south of Saint-Vith. An extension of the southern flank west of the River Our was manned by the 424th Infantry, the surviving regiment in the 106th Division. Another formation occupied a 'refused' or right angle position to the west intended to guard the end of this southern flank. That regiment was the 112th Infantry, the northernmost unit of the 28th Division.

The German forces opposing them were eager to drive on to the Meuse. These units included 18th and 62nd Volksgrenadier Divisions directly opposite the immediate vicinity of Saint-Vith and armoured formations to the north: Führer Begleit Brigade formed from the headquarters security, in addition to 9th SS Panzer Division, moved south from Sixth Panzer Army to advance more quickly to the west. The Volksgrenadiers also received support from a heavy panzer battalion of Tiger tanks.

The attack was launched in the afternoon of 21 December and although portions of the eastern line held, other areas were overrun, and during the evening tanks with infantry riding on their hulls entered the town. The Americans issued orders to form a defensive line on high ground west of town, but relatively few of the surviving defenders east of town successfully moved back.

Ultimately it was decided to withdraw all troops back across the River Salm through the narrow gap the 82nd Airborne defended between the towns of Vielsalm and Salmchâteau. Matthew Ridgway of XVIII Airborne Corps was placed in charge of the composite forces and was initially reluctant to retreat. His own observations and opinions of First Army staff and Field Marshal Montgomery in overall command of the northern forces came to favour a withdrawal. The roads were crowded and in poor condition, but a rapid drop in temperature on the night of 22–23 December froze muddy surfaces and greatly improved traction.[2]

The 28th Division moved to Luxembourg, in part to recover from terrible losses sustained in the Hürtgen Forest. The Fifth Panzer Army assault ploughed through the location and badly damaged the division commanded by Norman Cota, the inspirational leader on the western end of Omaha Beach during D-Day. The 112th Infantry in the north was involved with the defence of Saint-Vith. The 110th Infantry was spread out between numerous villages along the front and sustained heavy losses including large numbers of missing and captured. The commander of the 110th Infantry was captured. His replacement, Lieutenant Colonel Daniel Strickler, completed a depressing after-action report in early January which mentioned that the three battalions of the regiment continued to resist until they ceased to function as battalions.[3] The 109th Infantry occupied positions in the vicinity of 4th Division forces on the southern front of the German advance.

In the South

The role of the German Seventh Army was clearly defined in the operational plan for the Ardennes offensive. Four infantry divisions allotted to the army would cross the Rivers Our and Sûre (or Sauer) along the Luxembourg border to push into Belgium hopefully as far as the Meuse, thereby forming a defensive line against the American reaction from the south that would surely occur. Although artillery was provided for use against American batteries and troop positions, the entire army would be supported by a meagre number of about thirty self-propelled armoured assault guns and a few tanks.

The northern limit of the army area aligned with that of 109th Infantry and extended into the area of responsibility for the 12th Infantry of the 4th Division. Between these two regiments stood a portion of the 9th Armoured Division, the 60th Armoured Infantry Battalion. As was the case with other regiments, the companies were separated and often based in small villages that provided shelter. The 5th Parachute Division crossed the Our in boats against 109th Infantry positions and gained footholds on 16 December, at times bypassing smaller forward positions and moving into the rear. On the following day the 109th devoted efforts to aid Company E in its defence of a crossroads village: Fouhren. Enemy attacks were driven back but so were American efforts to resupply the company in the village.

The 352nd Volksgrenadier Division also crossed in boats and though held up at points the advance continued. The Our flowed into the River Sûre at Wallendorf. The division moved along the south bank of the Sûre but this movement was observed and subjected to punishing artillery fire. The same artillery aided the defenders of Fouhren. Eventually the batteries were driven from their firing positions. By the evening of the 17th anti-tank and assault guns moved across a new bridge to strengthen the attack of 5th Parachute Division. Another bridge was completed in the 352nd sector but movement remained slow.

By 18 December 5th Parachute Division moved west into the positions of the 110th Infantry and beyond the 109th area but the latter's battle with the 352nd continued. Nothing had been heard from the beleaguered company in Fouhren since late on the evening of the 17th when another company did not reach the village. A patrol on the morning of the 18th found only a burned command post and no sign of American troops.

The position of the 109th Infantry was sufficiently threatened that the regiment began a withdrawal to higher ground at Diekirch on the 18th. The 352nd struck the Diekirch position on the afternoon of the 19th and the regiment again fell back, this time to Ettelbruck, as much of the population abandoned their homes and headed south.

The 276th Volksgrenadier Division launched its attack across the Sûre against the 60th Armoured Infantry Battalion based in the town of Haller. They also moved into the steep gorge of the Ernz Noire that provided avenues inland and access to the rear of the 4th Division sector. Their initial artillery barrage fell on Beaufort and Haller. Infantry moved up the Ernz Noire gorge to surround Berdorf and the Parc Hotel where intrepid soldiers from the 12th Infantry held out. The gorge also provided access via crossing roads leading to towns such as Haller and Waldbillig.

Yet the failure to secure the heights west of the Sûre caused displeasure at Seventh Army headquarters. The flank dangers posed by movement up the Ernz Noire gorge led to unsuccessful efforts by Americans to drive the Germans out. Late on 17 December Beaufort was occupied. Falling back south from Haller, a defensive line was formed by 9th Armoured Division from Waldbillig near the gorge north-west to Ermsdorf. The commander of Seventh Army, Brandenberger, replaced the commander of 276th Division, Kurt Möhring, but the latter was killed by American fire before arrival of Oberst (Colonel) Hugo Dempwolff.

An American counter-attack attempted to reach three isolated companies of the 60th Armoured Infantry but was unable to do so. Eventually the companies received orders to do their best to move back through the German lines and slightly less than two-thirds did so.

The new division commander, Dempwolff, reorganized and rested his troops on the 19th then launched an assault on Waldbillig south from Haller and west out of the gorge on the 20th with a limited number of assault guns that finally arrived. American tank destroyers and artillery stopped the attacks from Haller but were ordered to withdraw south towards Christnach following assaults from the gorge coupled with the continued threat from Haller.[4]

Germans from the 212th Volksgrenadier Division began to cross the Sûre in force on 16 December, finding spread-out positions of the 12th Infantry companies. Despite communication difficulties due to telephone lines cut by artillery fire, American artillery in response fired on coordinates provided via radio with substantial effect. The 12th received some support from the depleted ranks of the 70th Tank Battalion, whose eleven Shermans in operating condition did not comprise a full company, and some available tank destroyer guns.

On the evening of 16–17 December the 2/22nd Infantry received word it would move early on the 17th, a tank company from 9th Armoured was available, additional artillery batteries were allocated and a portion of the 10th Armoured pried loose from Third Army would be sent to the area. On the second day of the offensive the Germans attempted to build a bridge into Echternach on ancient stone piers but were driven away and sought another location. The numerical advantage of German infantry would be offset by the armoured support available to the 4th Division. Company F of the 12th Infantry continued to hold the Parc Hotel in Berdorf despite being shelled by German artillery and American tank crews who thought the building was occupied by the enemy. One of the defenders, First Sergeant Gervis Willis, was awarded the Distinguished Service Cross for his role in the defence against infantry attacks.[5]

The armoured force from 10th Armoured, specifically Combat Command A, arrived in late afternoon with a plan: one group would advance in the Ernz Noire gorge, one from Consdorf to Berdorf, and the last would move to relieve Echternach, all beginning on the morning of 18 December. Tanks advancing down the gorge were stopped by firing positions in the rough cliffs on both sides. The middle group was stopped in Berdorf. The final one moved through Scheidgen to the outskirts of Echternach and informed Company E 12th Infantry to withdraw. The commander refused due to a no-retreat order he believed to be in effect.

Company E 8th Infantry attacked east from Waldbillig into the west side of the gorge on 19 December to ease the way for the tanks but was subjected to heavy artillery fire. This company would later be evaluated as sustaining the heaviest losses in the division. At one point command devolved upon a lieutenant who had only recently arrived as a replacement.[6] The force moving on Berdorf made some progress but the Germans reinforced their positions with rocket launchers and some armour.

American defenders in effect were serving as a shield to guard the eastern flank of Third Army as it began its northward advance. By the 20th the combat command from 10th Armoured served as a mobile reserve. During the night of the 19th the Germans also shifted to a defensive posture since their advance had achieved the objective of securing a position north of Luxembourg City.

Americans left Berdorf on the 20th and with armoured assistance those troops retired to a defensive line north and east of Consdorf. The final effort to reach Echternach on the same day was stymied at the edge of town. 10th Armoured recalled the tank force and Company E with some men from Company H surrendered. The Germans gained control of the roads from the Sûre in an area north of Luxembourg City but were lodged against an increasingly solid line of defence.[7]

*   *   *

The Line on the Northern Interior

The 82nd Airborne Division was preparing for the onset of winter in France when the commander James Gavin received notice on 17 December his division and the 101st Airborne would move eastward in response to the Ardennes offensive. As preparations were underway, the divisional staff assembled for a briefing at 8.00pm to learn the situation so far as it was known. Following the meeting, Gavin and a few staff officers drove in the dark through miserable weather east to First US Army headquarters in Spa, Belgium. During a meeting at 9.00am in the morning of the 18th, it was decided to deploy the 82nd to the Werbomont area west along one route to the River Meuse. The 101st Airborne would establish and hold a perimeter around the important crossroads town of Bastogne. Gavin reconnoitred the landscape and travelled as far south as Bastogne then joined the first elements of the 82nd arriving near Werbomont late on the 18th. All divisional units were assigned defensive positions shortly after dawn on the 19th.[8]

The 82nd first held a line between Trois-Ponts to the east and Werbomont to the west, but soon soldiers of the division would advance to occupy a U-shaped alignment southward past Trois-Ponts. Their major goal was holding a corridor between Vielsalm south to Salmchâteau through which troops in the Saint-Vith area could retreat westward. The Americans knew the decision to evacuate Saint-Vith was inevitable and as a consequence an escape corridor to the west was essential. The defensive line established by the 82nd extended west from Salmchâteau along a road through Baraque-de-Fraiture and beyond to a planned junction with 3rd Armoured Division. Since a complete junction was never achieved, the right flank of the division line remained a cause of concern during the early days of the operation.

The 82nd also worried about its rear areas. It will be recalled from the previous chapter that Kampfgruppe Peiper could not move west from Trois-Ponts and turned northward in search of other bridges and routes. An intact bridge across the Amblève south of La Gleize enabled elements of the kampfgruppe to cross and probe westward to and beyond the village of Cheneux.

Gavin and Reuben Tucker who commanded the 504th Parachute Infantry discussed evidence suggesting the Germans focused on moving through La Gleize towards 30th Division positions in Stoumont. The 82nd commanders decided to seize Cheneux and the small bridge across the Amblève. The 1st Battalion 504th attacked late on the 19th and early on the 20th with limited support from a captured enemy artillery piece. The two companies sustained heavy casualties but with assistance from two tank destroyers gained and held the western portion of the village. The following day – 21 December – a company from 3rd Battalion circled around to complete occupation of the village. Although some German Panzergrenadiers fell back across the bridge, most died or surrendered themselves along with their assault guns and anti-aircraft vehicles. The 1st Battalion companies were reduced to less than fifty men each; one – Company C – had less than twenty men and no officers. Although the division was proud of the achievement, MacDonald regarded the attack without adequate artillery support as too hasty, resulting in the high losses.[9]

Movement to the line west from Salmchâteau created a salient that would be unnecessary once troops to the east had fallen back from Saint-Vith. On 21 December Matthew Ridgway who commanded the American airborne corps informed Gavin they would likely withdraw to a line further to the north. Gavin objected but recognized defence of the salient would be costly and confer no advantage. Following reconnaissance and evaluation, a line from Trois-Ponts south-west to Manhay offered the best defensive positions. Troops from the 2nd SS Panzer Division were driven back from the south-west corner of the advance line but enemy pressure was increasing. The 82nd eventually withdrew to the northern line on the night of 24 December. Later it was learned that Kampfgruppe Peiper had begun to fall back to the south-east on the same evening after abandoning vehicles and leaving wounded behind in La Gleize. The 30th Division north of Trois-Ponts at La Gleize and Stoumont effectively stopped the advance of Kampfgruppe Peiper following bitter and desperate fighting.

The 82nd held the line south-west from Trois-Points against assaults during the last week of December. Along this line the collection of farm structures known as Erria was attacked on the night of 27 December by 9th SS Panzergrenadiers but troops from the 508th Parachute Infantry remained in position until relief arrived early on the 28th.

To Cross the Meuse

American divisions assembled in the north to attack the penetrating forces as Third Army began its assault from the south on 22 December. The northern force under the control of Joe Collins and VII Corps contained a cavalry group, the 75th and 84th Divisions, 2nd Armoured and some portion of 3rd Armoured Divisions. Montgomery wished to hold those units back and launch them in offensive action against the German flank, but penetrations made the reserve increasingly difficult to maintain. Indeed, Courtney Hodges of First Army needed them to hold important crossroads such as Marche on the highway leading from Bastogne to the Meuse.

The commander of Fifth Panzer Army, von Manteuffel, urged his subordinate commanders and their troops forward. The 2nd Panzer Division pushed patrols west on the night of 19–20 December and crossed the River Ourthe but paused due to fuel shortages. The reconnaissance battalion continued its advance once fuel arrived. The American 84th Division was also active, pushing screening elements south of Marche. A kampfgruppe from 2nd Panzer followed on the 23rd and after some delays decided to continue behind the reconnaissance troops, thereby bypassing Marche while leaving some Panzergrenadiers to cover a road leading to the town.

The American 2nd Armoured Division assembled at the same time on the 23rd north of Marche. That day an advance company followed by Combat Command A of the division moved south-west to occupy roads in the town of Ciney. A portion of the combat command headed south-east to Buissonville at night and while en route ambushed and shot up a German column in the village of Haid.

Most of Panzer Lehr Division began its drive to the Meuse from the Bastogne area on 22 December but was delayed by a lack of fuel until midday on the 23rd. Seeking to pass through Rochefort they encountered the 3rd Battalion of the 335th Infantry from 84th Division and fighting erupted that continued through the night. Having delayed the advance, the battalion received orders to withdraw and most soldiers were able to do so in vehicles or on foot. Although Lehr did not immediately advance – its soldiers needed rest – the division was located roughly 14 miles from Dinant on the Meuse.

Manteuffel realized the dangers inherent in pushing the two panzer divisions forward in essence with exposed flanks. However, support was expected from 9th Panzer Division and 15th Panzergrenadier Division although much of the latter remained behind to assault Bastogne. In addition, he would urge the 116th Panzer forward to cut across roads leading north from Marche, a task the division ultimately could not do in the face of opposition from the 84th Division.

The 2nd Panzer reconnaissance battalion continued to push forward with a kampfgruppe behind. Collectively the forces contained about forty tanks, twenty-five self-propelled guns and Panzergrenadiers. British armoured units were positioned ahead of bridges across the Meuse to give advance warning and provide time to demolish the bridges. The reconnaissance troops encountered one such advance guard from the 3rd Royal Tank Regiment on 24 December near the town of Foy-Notre-Dame, a few kilometres from the river. The British tanks opened fire, destroying a few vehicles in the column and generating such surprise the reconnaissance unit sought refuge in the town.

On that day the number of German armoured divisions apparently approaching or at least trying to reach the Meuse caused concern for Montgomery. Yet most were in greatly weakened conditions from earlier fighting, suffering from fatigue, supply shortages particularly of gasoline and air attacks during daylight. The Germans would not reinforce the drive until other units arrived to provide flank protection.

On Christmas Day the advance forces of 2nd Panzer were located in Foy-Notre-Dame and woods in the vicinity of the nearby town of Celles. Combat Command B in 3rd Armoured Division moved in and reduced positions near Celles then Foy-Notre-Dame, destroying vehicles and capturing prisoners in the process. On the evening of the 25th when a group from 9th Panzer arrived near Marche, much reduced armoured and infantry elements from 2nd Panzer and Lehr struggled forward. Both columns were beset on the 26th by American and British armour in addition to RAF Typhoons firing rockets. Given such opposition, both were ordered to retire to Rochefort.

The remnants of the 2nd Panzer advance element, at least those that had not already surrendered, abandoned tanks and other vehicles and some made their way back on foot, as had been the case with Kampfgruppe Peiper a few nights earlier. The maximum extent of the advance had been reached and fell just short of the Meuse.[10]

The Way Back

The lifting of the siege around Bastogne by no means represented the end of the threat to its garrison. Powerful German forces existed in the area and undertook concerted efforts to capture the town. On 30 December an attack by 11th Armoured and 87th Division ran headlong into the flank of a German advance from the north-west by Panzer Lehr and the 26th Volksgrenadier Division seeking to once again isolate Bastogne. On the opposite side of the town elements of 1st SS Panzer Division and 167th Volksgrenadier Division attacked two American infantry divisions, the 26th and 35th. Artillery and tactical air support assisted in halting these forces on a day Patton believed to be the crucial one of the operation. Repeated enemy attacks on the 31st were again thwarted as 6th Armoured advanced but American casualties were heavy, especially in 11th Armoured, considered 'very green' by the commander of Third Army.

By 1 January it was determined an enemy force in a wooded area south-east of Bastogne threatened the supply corridor into town. A plan was devised to send the 90th Division in to deal with these forces to the south-east, an effort that would be strongly supported by artillery. Another simultaneous attack was laid on for that day west of town by 4th Armoured and the 101st Airborne to supplement efforts by 87th Division and 17th Airborne with the general intention of moving northward in the direction of Houffalize. The collective effort by eight divisions began on 9 January. The 90th sustained heavy casualties from artillery but continued to advance as did 4th Armoured and the 101st in the general direction of Noville. The movement of 17th Airborne was hampered by casualties sustained during actions on previous days by the 513th and glider regiments.

Enter the 513th

Much of the 17th Airborne Division first experienced combat west of Bastogne with assignment to Third Army. One regiment in the division – the 507th – possessed a cadre of experienced soldiers since the unit jumped into Normandy with the 82nd Airborne on 6 June. The battle west of Bastogne in early January would be the introduction to combat for the 513th Parachute Infantry and two glider regiments in the division. This introduction was not an auspicious one.

An attack delayed by weather was finally launched on 4 January by the 513th from woods and high ground towards villages on the north side of the road leading to Bastogne. The purpose was an expansion of the defensive cordon around Bastogne and more generally to participate in the decimation of German troops within the salient. The 2nd Battalion crossed the road and one platoon advanced into the village of Flamizoulle but disappeared, presumably captured as they did not return. The 1st Battalion could not cross the road in the face of fire from artillery and self-propelled guns and gained shelter in a depression south of the road. The 3rd Battalion emerged from the wooded Bois de Fragotte (or Fragette) to fill the gap between the other battalions. One battalion – presumably the 1st – reported losses of 40 per cent in the attack on the 4th, a figure Patton found hard to believe. He later praised the individual performances of the men in the regiment but believed the high casualties arose from inexperience in the division.[11]

Another advance was ordered on 7 January. Three regiments would be employed: 194th Glider Infantry on the left (west), 513th moving on Flamierge in the centre and 193rd Glider Infantry attacking Flamizoulle on the right (east). The 1st and 2nd Battalions of the 513th pushed across the road but encountered strong resistance. The 3rd Battalion crossed the high ground and advanced into Flamierge where they remained through the evening. Since neither regiment on either flank moved forward as far, the 3rd Battalion position in particular was exposed.

The next morning (8 January) German armour and infantry launched attacks from two directions seeking to exploit this exposure. One force moved down the road from the north-west and wedged between the 2nd and 3rd Battalions. Other Germans struck west from Flamizoulle into the rear of the 1st and 2nd Battalions.

Both eventually fell back to the wooded area. The Third Battalion held on in Flamierge during the day, a position that became increasingly untenable. A withdrawal was ordered in late afternoon but communications difficulties with the troops in the village delayed evacuation until around midnight. The wounded were left in the village under care of medics, while those who could retired to Monty south of the road before dawn on 9 January. The rising ground leading north-west from the village of Monty to Flamierge including a rise south of the road opposite Flamierge would be known as 'Dead Man's Ridge' to the regiment.[12]

All soldiers remembered the cold and harsh winter conditions and Company A in the 513th was no exception. Ed Ballas, who received the Bronze Star Medal in the Ardennes and was known as 'Boss' to friends, commented his feet turned black – an indication of frostbite – and it was the only time he curled up with a man for warmth. Ralph Clarke who was wounded also had frozen feet and felt after the war 'my feet never get warm' although a decision to reside in Maine might have been another reason. He continued in later years to place shoes and socks near the stove to warm them. By contrast Irv Hennings grew up in Minnesota and played outside in zero temperatures so the winter cold in the Ardennes did not bother him.

Care of the wounded and recovery of the dead were challenging. One soldier, something of a legend due to his large size and because he viewed the company as his home, was badly wounded by a mortar shell and then shot by a rifleman as he moved on the ground. As a measure of likely unconscious apology, Germans troops transported him from the field to a hospital in Belgium where their doctors used clamps to bind his wounds. Later recovered by American soldiers, he spent about a year in military hospitals, receiving a plate in his skull and a metal replacement for a portion of his femur.

Hennings volunteered at one point to assist in recovering the dead. His team gathered the frozen bodies using a jeep and trailer, at times compelled to sit on the corpses if many were found. They unloaded bodies at crossroads locations where Graves Registration personnel – generally African American soldiers in his recollection – would collect them. Irv was not bothered by gathering the dead since they were beyond help but the wounded troubled him greatly.[13]

The Forces Unite

Concerns about a possible German counter-movement to the south near Saarbrücken led to the transfer of 4th Armoured to eventually join two other armoured divisions from the Meuse. Attacks resumed on 12 January with III Corps divisions on the verge of finishing off Germans still in the pocket south-east of Bastogne while the VIII Corps divisions (87th, 17th Airborne, 11th Armoured and 101st Airborne) continued the advance northward. Elements of 11th Armoured made contact at

Houffalize with those of 2nd Armoured from First Army at about 9.00am on 16 January, thus re-establishing a unified front within the area of German advance.

Movements in the latter half of January carried American forces back to towns once held in the fall of 1944. XII Corps commenced an advance north of Luxembourg City on 17 January into the southern flank of the German salient. Diekirch fell to 5th Infantry Division on the next day and corps units continued to move along the Rivers Sûre and Our in the direction of Saint-Vith. III Corps occupied Wiltz on the 22nd, Clervaux on the 25th, and by the 28th gained high ground overlooking Saint-Vith. Several days earlier on the 23rd Saint-Vith was entered by 7th Armoured units with First Army advancing from the north.[14]

The personal impact of attacks during harsh winter cold and snow is provided by considering the experiences of one company and battalion. Troops in the 101st who previously held defensive positions would now seek to advance against Germans fighting with the desperation of men holding open an escape route eastward. The 506th Parachute Infantry moved north with the division during the general advance by Third Army.

After days spent in woods enduring artillery fire, Company E from 2nd Battalion entered open fields on the morning of 13 January with support from Company I to capture the town of Foy astride the road north from Bastogne. Company E movement paused just short of Foy for a time due to confusion on the part of the company commander that increased the casualties sustained. The acting battalion commander, Major Richard Winters, sent First Lieutenant Ronald Speirs to relieve the indecisive commander and resume the attack. The town was largely secured by late morning but the advance had been costly with losses due to snipers and fire from machine guns and tanks. The twenty prisoners first seized indicated about twice that number from a company in 9th Panzer Division remained but even more eventually surrendered while others escaped to the north.

The 3rd Battalion moved in to hold Foy in mid-afternoon with support from Company F. However, early the next day (14 January) German tanks and infantry returned and American units were driven back to the high ground south of town by 6.00am. Three hours later an artillery concentration pounded Foy in preparation for another advance. Shortly afterwards Company I led 3rd Battalion back to the town. The 2nd Battalion circled beyond to the north in an advance to secure Cobru on the outskirts of Noville. The companies received mortar and artillery fire during the movement resulting in two killed and eight wounded. By 6.00pm the battalion was 'well in town' and organizing defensive positions. On the 15th the advance continued into Noville with support from 1st Battalion and armoured units that at first fired on the 2nd Battalion until informed of the presence of American troops. The occupation of Noville possessed a redemptive quality since early in the offensive the 1st Battalion assisted American armour defending the town on 19 and 20 December

– losing their commander Lieutenant Colonel James LaPrade in the action – before retiring south through Foy.

The 16th of January brought the occupation of yet another village, Rachamps, by 2nd Battalion. Positions held by the 101st would be assumed by the 17th Airborne beginning the following day and the 506th Parachute Infantry with the other components of the division shifted to a reserve area before movement south near Haguenau in Alsace. Company E entered the Ardennes with approximately 121 soldiers and came out with 63. Since the company received some replacements during the campaign, overall losses exceeded 50 per cent and included 11 killed.[15]

Command and Control

Montgomery assumed command of Bradley's troops north of the Bulge, effectively all of First Army. As the battle entered January the Field Marshal sought to retain control of both First and Ninth Armies. He once again raised the question of a single ground force commander controlling the American 12th and British/Canadian 21st Army Groups. He believed the German advance in the Ardennes was largely due to lack of a single leader and by extension the broad front approach emphasized by Eisenhower. Monty sent a letter to Eisenhower on 29 December stating he as commander of the 21st Army Group should be given full operational control over Bradley's 12th Army Group in a northern thrust to subjugate the Ruhr.[16]

Eisenhower and his Anglo-American staff at Supreme Allied Headquarters reached their limits. Ike prepared a telegram for the Allied Joint Chiefs essentially calling for the removal of Montgomery or his own replacement. Given the preponderance of American divisions on the continent, the choice seemed a clear one to the loyal staff at SHAEF.

Freddie de Guingand, Montgomery's chief of staff, sensed trouble and his suspicions were confirmed during a telephone call to SHAEF.[17] He travelled to Eisenhower's headquarters and asked the message be delayed until he could return and speak with Montgomery. His intervention – which included assisting Monty in preparing a message pledging full support for Eisenhower's strategy – prevented transmission of the telegram and defused a crisis that undoubtedly would have led to the dismissal of the Field Marshal. The press, both British and American, continued to stir controversy. De Guingand met with British representatives but with them his efforts were less successful. Bradley was of course stung by active or passive criticism despite his growing optimism. During the period from mid-December until mid-January, Bradley commanded only those forces south of the salient, meaning Patton's Third Army. He entered the fray following a Montgomery press briefing with his own conference, emphasizing the temporary nature of British direction of American forces in the north. He also informed Ike that neither he nor Patton would serve under Montgomery's command.

The End of the Bulge

Ultimately the Allies faced the decision of how to reduce the German salient into their lines. American military doctrine indicated such a penetration should be cut off at its base – provided sufficient forces existed to do so – compelling enemy troops within the salient to wither and surrender due to a lack of support and supplies. Patton favoured such an option, specifically an advance by Third Army north-east while First Army pushed south-east, with a junction point at the German town of Prüm. Joe Collins commanded VII Corps in First Army and was eager to drive from the northern shoulder south-east into the German flank. When Montgomery – perhaps thinking of Market Garden – questioned the wisdom of attempting to supply an entire corps along a single road from Malmédy to Saint-Vith, Collins said it would be no problem for the Americans.[18]

Such bold plans were rejected in favour of a more conservative exertion of pressure on all sides of the salient, not unlike what had occurred in Normandy at Falaise. An emphasis was placed on a central advance with Third Army forces moving northward from Bastogne and First Army divisions on the northern edge driving southward. They would meet at Houffalize on 16 January and operational control of First Army returned to Omar Bradley. The Ninth Army would remain with Montgomery.

By mid-January the 82nd Airborne entered a rest area in Nonceveaux, Belgium. Earlier in January the division returned to the line originally occupied in December. Troops crossed the River Salm and occupied the towns of Vielsalm and Salmchâteau, devastating the 62nd Volksgrenadier Division in the process. Nevertheless, the attack proved difficult until the 508th Parachute Infantry entered Thier du Mont and eliminated German observation points. Soldiers continued to be wounded and killed; Lieutenant Colonel Benjamin Vandervoort lost an eye while advancing near Arbre-fontaine and Captain Hugo Olson was wounded in the leg by shrapnel from a tree burst. Another soldier had a leg severed at the time but was saved by application of a tourniquet and morphine.

A lengthy diary entry by James Gavin ranged from the difficulties of winter campaigning through weapons evaluations to praise for his own men:

> Came close to getting shot at Grand Halleux when I had to dive into one of our own fox holes to avoid a schmeiser that was squirting in what a quick estimate led me to believe was my direction. Conditions have been very rugged. Temperature around 18°F, snow wind. It is amazing how these lads live sometimes. In all of my good paratroop units they attack in ordinary combat uniforms, hoping to bring up the overcoats and blankets later. Rations are cold entirely unless they can heat them in a hole if and when they get to one. Most regular outfits wear overcoats. Soldiers must be taught to be tough and in teaching them officers must set the example. There is a fundamental difference between

combat and manoeuvres. Combat is the payoff, there is <u>no</u> discomfort too great if it will bring victory in even the smallest fight. Most outfits bring up hot chow when they can which is frequently often. We eat cold chow entirely in the forward areas. Trench foot is a source of casualties in some cases greater than gun shot wounds. One Bn my 551 did not wear its overshoes in an attack and sustained about 230 trench foot cases in three days. Gun shot wounds and shrapnel were about 190. That Bn is comparatively ineffective now. We are now training with panzerfausts which are damn good. They will punch the front plate of a tiger tank. We are also training our men to drive tanks and tank destroyers since our armoured supporting people frequently abandon their vehicles when threatened in an attack. [The broad applicability of this statement seems unjustified.] Commanding this division is quite a task and a feat. I hope that I measure up to it well. These troops are the best in the world and are deserving of the best leadership. Given it they will do anything.[19]

Losses

Detailed accountings for a campaign composed of many separate battles during the harsh winter months presented a challenge. Figures offered by MacDonald summarize the magnitude of loss. The Americans devoted roughly 600,000 troops in opposition to the advance, with 81,000 becoming casualties including 19,000 killed and 15,000 prisoners of war. British forces fighting primarily at the western tip of the salient numbered another 55,000 with casualties around 1,400. German units encompassed roughly 500,000 men with perhaps 100,000 soldiers either killed, suffering wounds or surrendering to the Allies.[20]

Third Army losses in the Ardennes were the highest for any operation during the campaign in Europe: nearly 30,000 including more than 4,200 killed. Comparisons of several regiments in First Army revealed unit losses. The 38th Infantry defended the approaches to Rocherath; they lost 781 men including 409 reported missing during the campaign. The 393rd also defended the trails leading to the twin villages and reported losses of 920 soldiers with 141 of those missing. The 26th Infantry that held the positions at Domaine Bütgenbach lost 565 men including 95 missing. By contrast, the 110th Infantry in the 28th Division, largely overrun in Luxembourg to the south, reported 2,468 casualties, among them 1,302 missing and at least 846 prisoners.[21]

The failure of the Ardennes offensive to split the Allied armies and reach the supply port of Antwerp weighed heavily on the Germans. A lack of reality was reflected in the transcript of a late January 1945 OKW meeting. The discussion was wide ranging and included statements on the superiority of German armour. Such assessments were largely true but the Allies had devised means of coping technologically and tactically. Besides, even tanks with better armour and guns could not advance if crippled mechanically or when their fuel tanks were dry.

Another report during the meeting that Americans lost 85,000 men in January was a surprisingly accurate assessment of those killed, wounded and missing (either killed or captured) during the Ardennes Campaign. Hitler – either optimistically or sceptically – responded that the figure would represent half of the losses during the entire war. Perhaps the most surprising comments occurred at the end in the discussion about the feasibility of involving prisoners of war from the Western Allies in combat against the Red Army. Alfred Jodl proclaimed, 'Should we succeed in persuading the British and Americans to fight against the Russians, this will be a sensation.' Such fantasies were possibly derived from the numbers of Russian and Polish prisoners drawn into the Wehrmacht and the 'transfer' of support among nations such as Romania from the Axis to the Russians.[22] In this Jodl would be greatly disappointed.

A Sherman armed with the new 76mm gun near Fraineux ('Frandeux' in original caption) east of the River Meuse on 27 December. Curiously no snow covered the ground. This tank from 2nd Armoured Division was transporting soldiers from the 75th Division. While the gun was an improvement compared with the short-barreled 75mm, it still could not match the power of the German 75mm and 88mm guns (Bradley, *A Soldier's Story*, 322–3). Initially assembled in VII Corps to stage an attack on the German flank, 2nd Armoured, 75th and 84th Divisions and 3rd Armoured confronted advance elements of the offensive to prevent any crossings of the Meuse. (*NARA*)

(**Above**) The 82nd Airborne held an extended defensive line west of Trois-Ponts and the River Salm during late December. On the evening of 27 December the 508th Parachute Infantry in stone-walled farmhouses at Erria faced repeated attacks from infantry of the 9th SS Panzer Division. The 3rd Battalion was overrun but early next morning the position was restored by a nearby reserve company counter-attacking to reach battalion soldiers who remained in place (Gavin, *On to Berlin*, 241–3). Cunningham photographed the division commander James Gavin visiting the 3/508th near Erria on 29 December. *(NARA)*

(**Opposite, above**) A view facing southward of the farm buildings at Erria in 1999.

(**Opposite, below**) The 6th Armoured Division used white bed sheets for cover near Bastogne on 1 January. *(NARA)*

(**Above**) Petrony visited the 307th Airborne Engineers from the 82nd Airborne near Hierlot on 4 January. (*NARA*)

(**Opposite, above**) An anti-aircraft position defended a bridge on 4 January as photographed by Tesser. The Luftwaffe was more active during the campaign than previously experienced by most soldiers. (*NARA*)

(**Opposite, below**) The original caption indicated this Tiger B tank was abandoned near La Gleize when photographed on 4 January. A stencil added to the front revealed the vehicle became property of First US Army. The turret number 204 designated the fourth tank from headquarters platoon of the second company in the heavy panzer battalion attached to Kampfgruppe Peiper. (*NARA*)

(**Above**) Norbuth recorded an evocative image on the 6th of an infantryman in the Ardennes. Private Vernon Haught from the 325th Glider Infantry in the 82nd Airborne was returning after three hours on guard duty. (*NARA*)

(**Opposite, above**) The 70th Division to the south was attempting to drive out German forces that reoccupied the French town of Wingen. Howell photographed the effect of their artillery fire on 6 January. (*NARA*)

(**Opposite, below**) Company A of 290th Infantry in 75th Division advances through snow to Beffe north of La Roche in Belgium on 7 January. Note the photographer with the group. The division experienced combat for the first time in front of the nearby River Ourthe in Belgium. (*NARA*)

(**Opposite, above**) Petrony captured an image of members of the 1st Battalion of the 505th Parachute Infantry in the 82nd Airborne on 8 January. (*NARA*)

(**Opposite, below**) Rachline encountered the 3rd Battalion of the 507th Parachute Infantry on 9 January following a night of fighting near Bastogne. The regiment jumped into Normandy with the 82nd but entered the line with the 17th Airborne Division during the Ardennes Campaign. (*NARA*)

(**Above**) Battery B of the 376th Parachute Field Artillery fired a 75mm pack howitzer in support of 82nd Airborne operations along the River Salm on 9 January. These small artillery pieces could be disassembled and transported by airborne troops but were described as rather ineffective by some veterans (Keegan, *Six Armies*, 78). Still, a former airborne soldier defended their use since at times pack howitzers were all they had for artillery support. (*NARA*)

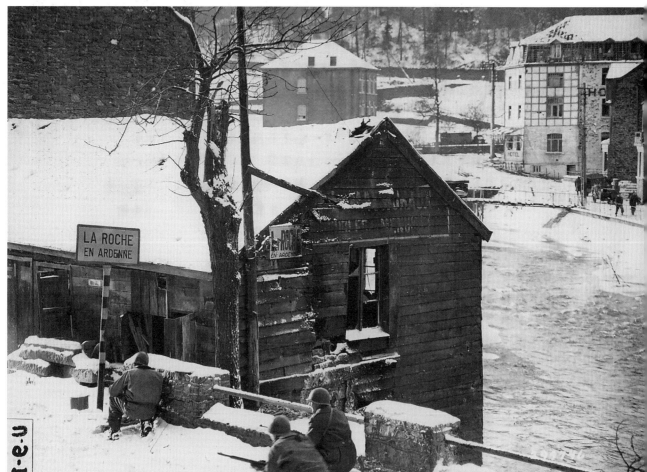

(**Opposite, above**) Lynch observed Company A of the 513th Parachute Infantry walking towards Marche in Belgium on 10 January. The second of two parachute regiments in the 17th Airborne Division, the 513th had experienced its first combat in the Ardennes west of Bastogne near Flamierge just a few days earlier and sustained heavy losses. (*NARA*)

(**Above**) Corporal Lloyd Hood 327th Glider Infantry in the 101st Airborne engaged in foot care on 11 January to prevent debilitating trench foot. A pair of rubber overshoes or galoshes would help but many soldiers found it impossible to maintain dry socks and feet when standing in snow or mud for prolonged periods. (*NARA*)

(**Opposite, below**) The 4th Cavalry Squadron cautiously entered La Roche-en-Ardennes, Belgium. Corrado travelled with the unit on 12 January as the Americans sought to regain town after town. (*NARA*)

(**Above**) A civilian walked amid the ruins of La Roche on 15 January. (*NARA*)

(**Opposite, above**) Allen moved with the 703rd Tank Destroyer Battalion on 13 January as Third Army advanced near Langlir between Houffalize and Vielsalm. The unit passed a Mark IV tank, designated the second in the second platoon (the company number was obscured). The date is confusing as Houffalize to the south was reached by Third Army units three days later. (*NARA*)

(**Opposite, below**) Roberts captured an image of Third Army vehicles on the road in Langlir the same day, 13 January. (*NARA*)

421456

283718

(**Opposite, above**) The 1st Battalion Headquarters Company from 309th Infantry of the 78th Division paused for a roadside meal near La Roche on that day, 13 January. The soldiers included (third through fifth right to left) Sergeant Russell LaBrasca and Private First Class John Vavrous from Pennsylvania, and James Sandifer from Georgia. Mr Sandifer (letter to National Archives 19 June 2008) indicated the unit served in the Hürtgen Forest in December. (*NARA*)

(**Opposite, below**) Graham encountered the 42nd Tank Battalion from the 11th Armoured Division near Longchamps north of Bastogne on 15 January. (*NARA*)

(**Above**) Soldiers from the First Army pushing down from the north met those from Third Army advancing north near Houffalize on 16 January. Hawkins was present to record the moment. (*NARA*)

(**Above**) Ellett observed the ruins in Houffalize on the next day, 17 January. (*NARA*)

(**Opposite, above**) A Panther fell upside down into a creek in Houffalize and was photographed on 20 January. (*NARA*)

(**Opposite, below**) After the war the Panther from the 116th Panzer Division was recovered and restored with camouflage paint and the number 401, denoting the first tank in the headquarters platoon of the fourth company.

(**Opposite, above**) Norbuth observed Company E 117th Infantry in the 30th Division in a field near Pont, Belgium, on 17 January. (*NARA*)

(**Above**) Lapine recorded an aerial image of the 6th Armoured Division advancing north-east of Bastogne on 18 January. The image depicts vehicles, their tracks in the snow, and shell holes as the division advanced against opposition. (*NARA*)

(**Opposite, below**) A Sherman tank was put out of action during the 6th Armoured movement through Mageret near Bastogne. Sher captured the image on 15 January. (*NARA*)

(**Opposite, above**) Company G of the 23rd Infantry in the 2nd Division crawled along a fence on the edge of a snowy field near Ondenval, Belgium, on 16 January. (*NARA*)

(**Opposite, below**) A gun from the 333rd Anti-Tank unit in the 83rd Division occupied a defensive position down a long lane near Bovigny, Belgium, on 17 January. (*NARA*)

(**Above**) The vulnerability of American armour was reflected in this view of anti-tank shell penetrations on the side of Sherman 'Concerto in C' near Etienne, Belgium. Rachline photographed soldiers studying the six holes on 16 January. (*NARA*)

(**Opposite, above**) The 82nd Airborne tested anti-tank weapons such as American bazooka and German Panzerfaust rockets for effectiveness in La Gleize. One tank covered with snow stood at left while the soldiers fired at the front armour of another, probably a Tiger. The Panzerfaust, using the shaped charge principle for its projectiles, was considered the superior weapon. Petrony recorded the scene on 18 January. (*NARA*)

(**Opposite, below**) Gilbert obtained an excellent image on 19 January of the 101st Engineers in the 26th Division marching across a field near Wiltz, Luxembourg. (*NARA*)

(**Above**) The 17th Airborne moved through the snow as recorded by Mallinder on 21 January. (*NARA*)

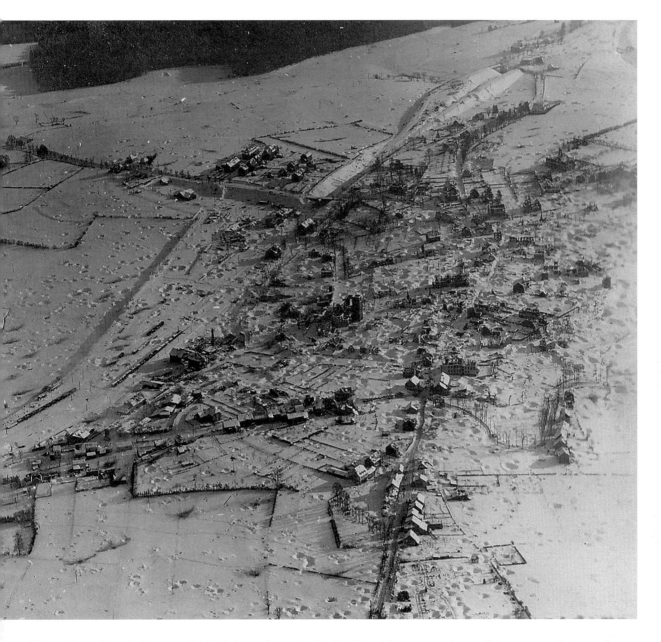

(**Opposite, above**) Company I 16th Infantry from the 1st Division riding on a tank near Schoppen south-west of Büllingen on the same day, 21 January. (*NARA*)

(**Opposite, below**) An aerial view of Wiltz by Zinni on 22 January. The 28th Division occupied the town in the Ardennes until the German offensive in mid-December overran their positions and compelled them to withdraw. (*NARA*)

(**Above**) An aerial view of Saint-Vith by Cravens on the same day, the 22nd. The 106th Division and troops from 7th Armoured Division held the town against the Germans until late December. Saint-Vith was recaptured on 23 January by the 7th Armoured Division in First Army as the German salient or 'bulge' was rapidly being eliminated. (*NARA*)

(**Opposite, above**) McHugh accompanied the 23rd Infantry Battalion from 7th Armoured into Saint-Vith on the 23rd. The solders wore white camouflage outfits and were concerned about snipers. (*NARA*)

(**Opposite, below**) The 75th Infantry advances near Saint-Vith on 23 January as photographed by Vetrone. (*NARA*)

(**Above**) Newhouse visited the ruins of a small church in Saint-Vith on 7 February. (*NARA*)

(**Opposite, above**) Company E 117th Infantry of the 30th Division occupied a position in Sart-lez-Saint-Vith just west of Saint-Vith on 23 January. *(NARA)*

(**Opposite, below**) McHugh photographed an image of 7th Armoured Division forces amid the ruins of Saint-Vith on 24 January. *(NARA)*

(**Above**) Shermans from the 40th Tank Battalion of the 7th Armoured Division occupied a field near Saint-Vith on the 24th. *(NARA)*

(**Above**) Cravens recorded another aerial image on the 21th near Saint Vith, this one showing tanks on a recent battlefield near woods. (*NARA*)

(**Opposite, above**) Hugh McHugh was attached to the 7th Armoured Division when he captured this image near Wallerode on the 25th. He was killed shortly afterwards and the film was retrieved by another soldier who was wounded. (*NARA*)

(**Opposite, below**) The multiple barrels of the *Nebelwerfer* launched rocket projectiles referred to by the Allies as 'screaming meemies' that would land with devastating effect on infantry positions. Schneider photographed an abandoned launcher in Luxembourg on 23 January. (*NARA*)

(**Above**) Company B of 325th Glider Infantry headed to Herresbach, Belgium, north-east of Saint-Vith on 28 January. (*NARA*)

(**Opposite, above**) Other elements of the 82nd Airborne Division in the snow near Herresbach on the same day, the 28th. (*NARA*)

(**Opposite, below**) Makarewicz was present as the 505th Parachute Infantry moved under fire into the town of Amel between Saint-Vith and Büllingen on 28 January. (*NARA*)

Petrony spent a cold day with the commander of the 82nd Airborne James Gavin while the latter was on a field telephone near Herresbach on the 28th. (NARA)

Members of the 508th Parachute Infantry marched to Holzheim southwest of Büllingen on 30 January. (NARA)

254002

Two Germans wearing American uniform items were captured near Snamont on 1 January 1945. Some Germans attempted to infiltrate positions and prevent bridge demolitions by posing as American soldiers. The combination of uniform items suggest these young soldiers were simply seeking protection from the cold. *(NARA)*

Petrony photographed a group of German prisoners being processed by the 82nd Airborne on 3 January. *(NARA)*

Roberts encountered a young German prisoner who was probably wounded and being transported on the hood of a jeep on 6 January. *(NARA)*

Sergeant Clarence Mageries from the 83rd Division guarded two prisoners described as members of a Waffen-SS unit at Sart, Belgium, on 9 January. *(NARA)*

(**Above**) Prisoners in the Belgian town of Sainlez were instructed to pile belongings by soldiers from the 90th Division on 13 January. (*NARA*)

(**Opposite, above**) Roberts photographed a young Waffen-SS prisoner of the 3rd Armoured Division on 15 January. (*NARA*)

(**Opposite, below**) Another young prisoner from the same parachute division appeared more pleased his war had come to an end. He was photographed in Weywertz on 15 January by Augustine. (*NARA*)

(**Right**) The enigmatic expression of a young prisoner from the 3rd Fallschirmjäger (Parachute) Division was also photographed in Weywertz, Belgium, by Augustine on the same day. (*NARA*)

(**Below, left**) This soldier on the 15th near Weywertz was a prisoner of the 1st Division. (*NARA*)

(**Below, right**) Manpower challenges facing the Wehrmacht before the offensive were reflected in the next two Augustine photographs near Bütgenbach on 24 January. This prisoner of the 26th Division was 37 years old and had been in military service for only nine months. (*NARA*)

This prisoner was 27 years old and had been in naval service since the late 1930s but was transferred to the Wehrmacht several months before the offensive. (*NARA*)

199685

(**Above**) These German prisoners of the 9th Infantry in the 2nd Division on 30 January in Büllingen seem glad to be done with the winter campaign. The 9th Infantry initially held the line east of the twin villages of Rocherath and Krinkelt when the Germans advanced on 16 and 17 December. (*NARA*)

(**Opposite, above**) Refugees on the road near Remiville near Bastogne were photographed by Meyer on 14 January. (*NARA*)

(**Opposite, below**) Allen observed family members walking along a road as they returned home to Lierneux, Belgium, on 16 January. (*NARA*)

This resident of La Roche waited to discover if her child buried in the rubble of a home has survived. A First Army photographer recorded the scene on 13 January. (*NARA*)

On another part of the front a French mother prepared to evacuate her children from Haguenau as elements of the American Seventh Army pulled back from the town on 20 January. (NARA)

Civilians with a precious cow returned to the village of Sart-lez-Saint-Vith, also known as Rodt, on 26 January. (NARA)

(**Above**) Newhouse observed a Red Cross worker Marjorie Wiegland from Wisconsin offering chewing gum to children in Saint-Vith on 10 February. Soldiers shared baked or roasted turkeys with residents of Luxembourg and Belgium during the Christmas season. Most had never encountered turkey but must have enjoyed both the smell and taste. (*NARA*)

(**Opposite, above**) Members of Company H 119th Infantry in the 30th Division transport some of their wounded in the vicinity of Saint-Vith on the 13th. (*NARA*)

(**Opposite, below**) The 325th Glider Infantry from the 82nd Airborne prepares to evacuate wounded from Herresbach as photographed by Petrony on 29 January. The heavy snowfalls in January resulted in dependence on tracked weasels to move supplies and evacuate wounded. (*NARA*)

(**Opposite, above**) Lapine witnessed a dead German in a field at Neffe near Bastogne on 3 January. The raised arm was frequently observed on battlefield dead. (*NARA*)

(**Opposite, below**) American soldiers who died in the fighting near Bastogne arranged in a row for a Graves Registration unit. Meyer photographed the scene on 11 January. (*NARA*)

(**Above**) A German soldier frozen along the road near Langlir was visible on 13 January. (*NARA*)

(**Above**) A German cemetery covered with snow near La Plez in Belgium on 5 January. (*NARA*)

(**Opposite, above**) A lone German grave and abandoned Panther tank stand out on the snowy landscape near Recht on 21 January. (*NARA*)

(**Opposite, below**) The winter snows covered American graves in Épinal, France. Lapidus photographed the scene on 12 January. (*NARA*)

General Patton visited the 87th Division on 30 January. (*NARA*)

General Troy Middleton of VIII Corps visited the front on 28 January in this Mallinder photograph. (*NARA*)

The harsh winter conditions were encapsulated in this image of a 79th Division soldier, T/5 John Brown from Brooklyn on 30 January. (*NARA*)

Private Joseph Klem from Olyphant, Pennsylvania, and the 357th Infantry in the 90th Division paused below an impromptu sign painted by Germans during the advance near Binsfeld in Luxembourg. Anders photographed him on 31 January. *(NARA)*

Soldiers from Company K in the 38th Infantry of 2nd Division kept a low profile in a field near Krinkelt on 31 January. *(NARA)*

Members of Company E, 23rd Infantry in the 2nd Division, moving eastward from Krinkelt on 31 January. Orange circles on the backs of snow capes served to identify members of the units; in the snow it was difficult to distinguish friend from foe. The northern portion of the German offensive began six weeks earlier just east of the twin villages of Rocherath and Krinkelt. *(NARA)*

A view in 2001 from the line held by 9th Armoured Division troops looking north in the general direction of the village of Haller in Luxembourg. Soldiers from the German Seventh Army on the southern edge of the offensive advanced across these fields into artillery firing from this line on 20 December.

German cemetery at Recogne looking south to fields beyond in the direction of Bastogne in 1999.

Luxembourg American Cemetery at Hamm contains 5,076 graves, many from the fighting in the Ardennes.

The German cemetery of Sandweiler, located close to the American one at Hamm, holds 10,913 graves, again mostly from the Ardennes offensive.

Chapter Three

Advance to the Rhine

As the Americans and British moved forward through late winter they began to occupy that portion of Germany west of the Rhine. The British in particular viewed crossing the Rhine as entry into the Reich. Observing airborne landings across the river on 24 March Montgomery asked Churchill when British forces last fought on 'German soil'. The prime minister responded that a rocket artillery brigade participated in the battle near Leipzig against Napoleon in October 1813.[1]

The pressure and fatigue during the Ardennes operations may have prompted James Gavin to express extreme frustration once the 82nd moved into a reserve area in Belgium. His comments likely reflected difficulties in moving exhausted troops forward during the winter cold, particularly when many replacements – officially termed 'reinforcements' for morale purposes – entered the line:

> If our infantry would fight this war would be over by now. On our present front there are two very weak german regts holding the XVIII Corps of four divisions. We all know it and admit it and yet nothing is being done about it. American infantry just simply will not fight. No one wants to get killed, not that anyone else does but at least others will take a chance now and then. Our artillery is wonderful and our air corps not bad. But the regular infantry, terrible. Everyone wants to live to a ripe old age. The sight of a few germans drives them to their holes. Instead of being imbued with an overwhelming desire to get close to the german and get him by the throat they want to avoid him if the artillery has not already knocked him flat. This is the fault of our training. Our paratroop infantry is superb, close quarters killers.[2]

Snow began to melt in early February and the ground surface returned to mud as Gavin examined a portion of the Hürtgen Forest battlefield from the previous fall. Such places were not pleasant to visit after three months.

> The snow has melted uncovering many of the dead and decayed of the past several months on this front. The 28th Division evidently took a bad beating in this area. A discouraging sight to see. Much of their tanks, jeeps, weasels, arms etc. abandoned. Their wounded and dead left on the ground now rotting. If only

our statesmen could spend a minute hugging the ground under mortar fire next to a three months old stiff. We just simply have got to stop war.[3]

*　　*　　*

The British 21st Army Group planned a double attack in February to drive to the Rhine from Nijmegen south to Düsseldorf. British and Canadian troops would advance through the Reichswald and across low lying land between the Rivers Maas and Rhine. The American Ninth Army would cross the River Roer, an event that had been a goal since late fall of the previous year. First Army with Bradley's 12th Army Group would cooperate to the extent of advancing on the right flank of Ninth Army towards Cologne. In the process they sought to gain control of the Roer dams before the Germans released water to flood the river valley.

British XXX Corps commanded by Brian Horrocks began the advance known as Operation Veritable south and east into the Reichswald on 8 February. Canadian II Corps under Guy Simonds joined the left flank to move through flooded lowlands parallel with the Rhine about a week later. Terrain and weather were appalling and German resistance on the whole solidified after the first few days. Distances between the Mass and Rhine varied from 2 miles to roughly 20 miles but movement for the most part passed through dense woods or open fields and villages between the rivers. Herculean efforts coupled with ample artillery and aerial support when weather permitted enabled the infantry and armour to clear much of the west bank of the Rhine as far as Xanten by 5–8 March.[4]

The area allocated to Ninth Army known as Operation Grenade was flooded as Germans opened relief valves on the dams to create a steady flow of flood waters. The attack would finally begin to cross the Roer on the night of 22–23 February. Progress was reasonably steady and movement was aided by the First Army advance protecting the right flank of Ninth Army. There were hopes at least one bridge across the Rhine might be seized near Düsseldorf but all were destroyed. Still, William Simpson who led Ninth Army urged Montgomery around 5–6 March to force a crossing below Düsseldorf. The commander of 21st Army Group remained focused on the major effort being planned near Wesel and divisions in British Second Army arranged themselves along the Rhine for that purpose.

The battles of the Rhineland cost British and Canadian forces 15,500 soldiers during the month. Ninth Army in seventeen days of action sustained casualties numbering slightly less than 7,300. German losses in defence were estimated at 90,000 including 51,000 prisoners. Another loss was Field Marshal Gerd von Rundstedt who was replaced as commander in the west for the final time by Hitler.[5]

At the end of January, Third Army arranged three of its corps from north to south, with the main effort provided by VIII Corps directed on Prüm within the defences of the Siegfried Line. A general order from 12th Army Group to maintain a posture of 'aggressive defence' on 7 February nonetheless allowed the attack on Prüm to continue. The return to conditions similar to those in the fall of 1944 led Third Army to conclude SHAEF was again favouring the northern advance of the British/Canadian forces and Ninth US Army under the direction of Montgomery. Troops from the 22nd Infantry of 4th Division entered Prüm on 11 February gaining control of the city the next day. At that point VIII Corps joined others in the renewed defensive phase.

Troops such as those from 17th Airborne and 6th Armoured Divisions still undertook patrols into German territory and the Siegfried Line. On 8 February, one such patrol from 2nd Battalion, 513th Parachute Infantry advanced across the River Our into Germany. Near the small village of Affler, the patrol encountered German positions and movement was halted by enemy fire. The patrol leader, First Lieutenant John Leary from Headquarters Company, was wounded and ordered the remaining members to fall back as he provided covering fire. The patrol moved back across the river but Lieutenant Leary did not join them. He was declared missing in action, receiving the Silver Star and later the Bronze Star Medal for his selfless actions.[6]

XX Corps began to clear the triangle formed by the confluence of the Rivers Saar and Moselle in mid to late February. The 10th Armoured and 94th Divisions moved northward to Trier on the Moselle that was cleared of enemy troops on 2 March. The 'aggressive defence' restriction was lifted in early March and shortly afterward 4th Armoured Division with a regiment of 5th Division carried in trucks began its 'historic dash' to the Rhine, travelling 50 miles in three days to reach the western bank on 8 March. The balance of XII Corps began advancing to the river during March.

Another division, the 11th Armoured, headed for the Rhine on 7–8 March and arrived two days later. Third Army concluded that its route was eased to a degree by disorganization among German ranks resulting from the earlier movement. One of the benefits arising from these rapid advances was the encirclement of German forces in the Eifel that represented a reversal of fortunes. From early March, VIII Corps divisions engaged in reduction of all enemy forces west of the Rhine.[7]

During 13–22 March Third Army moved east into the Saar industrial region, occupying cities and establishing contact with Seventh Army on 20 March west of Kaiserslautern. Such movement was essentially what was planned in December before the German offensive in the Ardennes. By late March control of the west bank of the Rhine within the zone of responsibility had been achieved. The 10th and 12th Armoured Divisions advanced 80 miles in three days to reach the Rhine at Ludwigshafen on 21 March. Attention then turned to sealing a narrow gap during the next two days to cut off the last escape route for German troops. More than 80,000 men were captured, representing remnants from much of First and Seventh Armies.[8]

The Remagen Bridge
The US First Army had also been active on the western approaches to the Rhine and a spectacular advance by 9th Armoured Division culminated in discovery of the

undestroyed Ludendorff railroad bridge across the river at Remagen on 7 March. Combat Command B of the division crossed and secured the span. There were some at Supreme Headquarters – not including Eisenhower – who devalued the achievement since it did not fit into the overall strategic 'plan' for a march through Germany.

As it happened, General Harold 'Pinky' Bull from SHAEF visited Bradley's 12th Army Group headquarters as seizure of the Ludendorff bridge unfolded. He immediately reminded Bradley that a major effort from the southern Rhine was contrary to the master plan for operations in the north, the plan for which Bull was a major strategist. Bradley said men and material would be pouring across to enlarge the bridgehead to push enemy artillery out of range of the bridge. He said they did not wish to change the plan, simply provide SHAEF with options for alternative operations or at least a diversion.

Bull remained unimpressed, saying any such operations would take too long to develop. An added complication was the belief in Ninth Army serving with Montgomery that it could cross in their sector then since opposition seemed completely disorganized. The discussion back and forth between Bull and Bradley with his staff continued into early the next day.

Hansen felt the issue reflected the 'inability and inflexibility of higher headquarters to adjust themselves rapidly to changes resulting from exploitation not foreseen in their plans.'[9] In other words, he expressed the idea of Patton emphasized by Liddell Hart that plans should adapt to conditions.

The plan was a northern 'set piece' advance up to the Rhine with infantry and armour. During the evening of 23 March 51st Highland Division from XXX Corps crossed in boats near the town of Rees. The 1st Commando Brigade from the British XII Corps moved over shortly afterward about 2 miles downriver from Wesel, a town shortly to be pounded by planes from Bomber Command. Early on the morning of 24 March 15th Scottish Division from XII Corps began crossing at Xanten near Wesel and would be the first ground forces to meet the airborne soldiers. Two American infantry divisions – 30th and 79th – from Ninth Army crossed south of Wesel also early in the day on the 24th. Some armoured units moved tanks over on vessels or by 'swimming' them as Duplex Drive vehicles.[10]

The crossings would receive support from the British 6th and American 17th Airborne Divisions. The 6th jumped into Normandy on 6 June 1944 at the eastern end of the Allied landing zone. The 17th fought in Belgium as infantry during January. Operation Varsity on 24 March would be the final major airborne effort of the war.

'Doing something to enhance you'

When one asked veterans why they volunteered for paratrooper training they generally would say for the extra pay. Following an era of economic depression that was a believable response. However, the men possessed an inherent desire to see if one could pass through the rigorous selection process. The minimum weight require-ment of 125lb could be overcome. The weight entries for Hal Green and another soldier were simply changed on their evaluation forms. Discipline was rigid but Stanley Morrison grew up accustomed to following orders and had no difficulty doing so in the army. Hal commented they were in superb condition because they ran everywhere. Ralph Clarke came to realize various forms of punishment at Fort Benning such as frequent push-ups actually meant you were always 'doing something to enhance you' in a physical sense.

Paratroopers were expected to complete five qualifying jumps in training. Bob Haight noticed the not-so-subtle pressure to continue. A training sergeant told them after the first jump there would be another tomorrow and if anyone was 'low enough and yellow enough to quit' they should do so. Hal Green was badly injured during his final qualifying jump and spent months in a hospital. He never made it to Europe.

Clarke remembered sitting in a shed waiting to board a plane for his first jump. He asked who had previously flown and no one raised a hand. Ralph thought it strange they would all shortly board a plane only to jump out of it. Following their successful first jump Ralph was walking along a road with his friend O'Daniel who suddenly said, 'Don't look up.' Some distance after passing a general and lady standing in a jeep, an agitated O'Daniel explained they were his father (John O'Daniel Sr.) and mother who had come out as witnesses. Ralph had two other close friends in training – Phillips and Eigel – and upon graduation all were assigned to different airborne units. He entered the orderly room to request they serve together. The sergeant replied, 'This is not a g** d*** social club,' and the assignments remained. John O'Daniel Jr. was killed in Holland serving with the 505th Parachute Infantry.

Herb Anderson taught marksmanship at the Fort Benning infantry school. Initially denied permission to join the airborne he was later allowed to do so; he thought due to a decree from President Roosevelt that all such requests could not be denied. During the Ardennes Campaign he served with the 513th Headquarters Company. After the Ardennes the regimental colonel relieved a company commander who Herb considered a good officer. Company A 513th Parachute Infantry would jump across the Rhine on 24 March with Captain Anderson in command.[11]

Another Crossing

On 22 March Gavin anticipated several crossings of the Rhine, in addition to offering a private observation on a famous war correspondent who had written about him in the fall of 1944:

> Well, Miss Gelhorn turned out to be quite a person. I have never met her likes and would just as soon not in anyone else … The staff gossip is that the Germans have practically no organized resistance on the far side of the Rhine.

The crossing is to be made by Montgomery on the 24th. His technique is interesting. His patience and thorough buildup is extremely conservative but undoubtedly what it takes in this kind of fighting. Patton is roaring along on the southern front and may cross the Rhine today and to hell with an airborne bridgehead. That is good fighting.[12]

In a move clearly intended to upstage Montgomery the American Third Army crossed the Rhine further south with much less fanfare a few days before Operation Varsity. The army staged the first 'assault' crossing – as opposed to the earlier seizure of Ludendorff bridge in Remagen by First Army – on the night of 22–23 March. A portion of the 5th Infantry Division with the support of amphibious Shermans from the 748th Tank Battalion crossed the river at Oppenheim. By noon on the 23rd the entire 5th Division arrived on the east bank, followed by the 90th Division and one combat command of the 4th Armoured Division. Engineers placed two bridges across the river within thirty-six hours. On 24 March – the day Varsity began – the 6th Armoured and 26th Divisions were across the Rhine while 4th Armoured progressed 20 miles beyond the river.

Gedricks photographed a newly-arrived American M24 light tank in Petit-Thier, Belgium, on 4 February. The tank had a torsion bar suspension and mounted a 75mm gun. A medium M26 tank armed with a 90mm gun also appeared, but not in sufficient quantities to replace the standard Sherman. (NARA)

(**Above**) The American armies moved forward from Belgium into Germany after pushing the Germans out of the 'bulge' resulting from the Ardennes offensive. Truck convoys crossed the River Our near Steffeshausen, Belgium, on 5 February as recorded by Mallinder. (*NARA*)

(**Opposite, above**) Mud became a hindrance to motorized advance as indicated by this truck nearly swallowed near Steffeshausen on the same day, 5 February. (*NARA*)

(**Opposite, below**) Third Army 59th Field Hospital at Schönberg in the Eifel east of Saint-Vith on 23 February. The staff included, from left to right, Lieutenants Marjorie Smart and Muriel Zimmerman assisted by Private First Class Benny Cruz. (*NARA*)

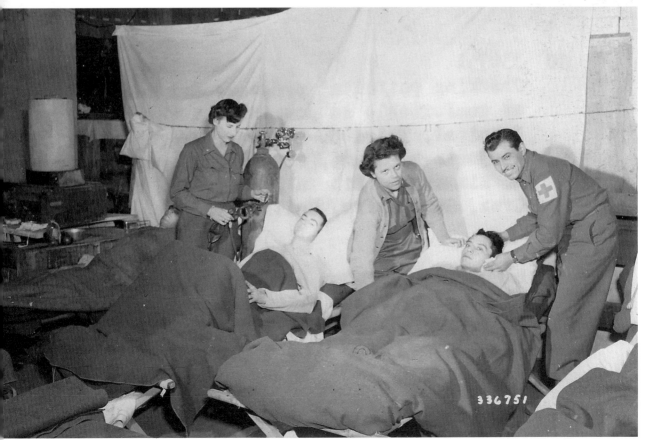

336751

(**Above**) An infantryman with the 84th Division paused north-east of Geilenkirchen in the town of Baal, Germany, on 24 February. The original caption for this Tesser photo noted that most of the locations on the sign across the road were in Allied hands. *(NARA)*

(**Opposite, above**) First Army seized the Ludendorff railroad bridge across the Rhine at Remagen in early March. This view from a railroad tunnel on the east bank leading to the bridge was recorded on 11 March. *(NARA)*

(**Opposite, below**) Fleming observed a smokescreen laid down on the Rhine at Rolandseck near Remagen on 19 March, presumably to provide cover for a planned operation. Similar smokescreens were used to cover infantry crossings on 24 March during Operation Varsity but caused problems for the airborne troops since some landing and drop zones were obscured. *(NARA)*

(**Above**) The 109th Field Artillery Battalion of the 28th Division serving with Third Army shelled Leutesdorf on 20 March. (*NARA*)

(**Opposite, above**) The mortar section from the 1st Battalion 318th Infantry of the 80th Division with Third Army fired on enemy positions in Neustadt before reaching the Rhine. Romero photographed the scene on 22 March. (*NARA*)

(**Opposite, below**) Halkias observed the surrender of citizens in Frankenthal to the 4th Armoured Division in Third Army on the same day, 22 March. (*NARA*)

(**Above**) Jones witnessed movement of First Army trucks across the Rhine at Linz near Remagen on 22 March. (*NARA*)

(**Opposite, above**) American armoured forces were acutely aware of the vulnerability of Shermans to enemy tank and anti-tank guns. Blau observed a Sherman in Steinfeld, Germany, on 23 March with cement bags used to provide added protection. (*NARA*)

(**Opposite, below**) The 78th Division passed through the ruins of Uthweiler on 23 March. (*NARA*)

Patton slipped elements of Third Army across the Rhine quietly before Operation Varsity to the north was launched. Nestareck recorded images of LCVP (landing craft vehicles personnel) carrying troops from the 5th Division across the river at Nierstein near Oppenheim on 23 March. (NARA)

Sullivan photographed the 87th Division in Third Army crossing the Rhine at Boppard on 25 March. (NARA)

(**Opposite, above**) Gilbert travelled with the 76th Division of Third Army on the east side of the Rhine in Bingen on 25 March. (*NARA*)

(**Opposite, below**) A jeep was loaded on a glider at an airfield near Coulmiers west of Orléans, France, on 21 March during preparations for Operation Varsity. (*NARA*)

(**Above**) The next day, 22 March, Forney witnessed a group of 'Apaches' with shaven heads from the 194th Glider Infantry of the 17th Airborne Division. (*NARA*)

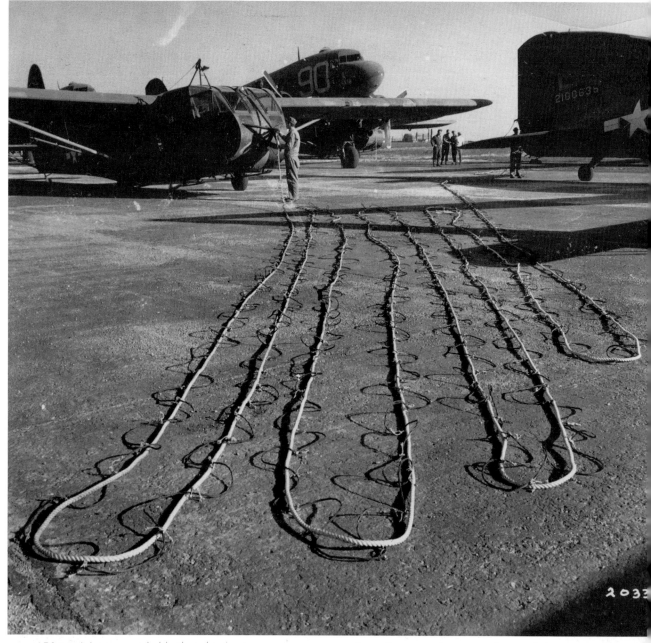

(**Above**) Forney probably thought the tow rope arrangement on the ground possessed an artistic appearance. (*NARA*)

(**Opposite, above**) Forney recorded this image of C-47 tow planes and gliders on the day before the operation. (*NARA*)

(**Opposite, below**) Arnowitz observed columns of C-47 transports lined up on a runway at Field A-50 near Orléans on 23 March. (*NARA*)

203325

Paratroopers consumed their 'last meal in France' on the afternoon/evening of the 23rd. *(NARA)*

Chapter Four

Varsity

Tactical planners – not wishing to repeat the distances between airborne and ground forces of Market Garden in Holland the previous fall – placed landing areas in the vicinity of Wesel just a few miles ahead of the British Second Army, albeit on the opposite side of the Rhine. Supporting British divisions crossed the river and made contact with paratroopers the same day while the American 30th and 79th Divisions crossed to the south of Wesel. The daylight operation should have resulted in a high percentage of accurate arrivals on jump and landing zones. However, unlike Market Garden, Varsity was not a surprise to the German defenders positioned near Wesel on the east bank of the Rhine. In addition, smoke generated to shield troops crossing the river in boats also served to obscure some of the landing zones, resulting in poor visibility for glider pilots.

One American, John Kormann, was filled with trepidation when he learned his section of the 517th Airborne Signal Company would land in a glider carrying a jeep and gasoline cans. Paratroopers knew flying and landing in a glider was a more dangerous means of entering combat than jumping from a transport. The results of 24 March would in part justify these fears.

*   *   *

Operation Varsity combined elements of previous major airborne efforts in north-west Europe. The Normandy airborne invasion, while launched along portions of a heavily-defended coastline, took place on a moonlit night so reactions of defenders were somewhat suppressed. Market Garden occurred during the daylight of a September afternoon but German forces were caught by surprise and initial reactions were again muted. Allied troops who jumped or landed across the Rhine in March 1945 would do so again in daylight, but in this instance the drop and landing zones were for the most part closely defended. The patient build-up of forces from the 21st Army Group on the west side of the river had aroused suspicion. Enigma data indicated German intelligence thought an airborne assault on the edge of the Rhine between Wesel and Duisburg was probable.[1]

The British 6th Airborne Division boarded transport planes or gliders at bases spread across England while the American 17th Airborne did the same at numerous

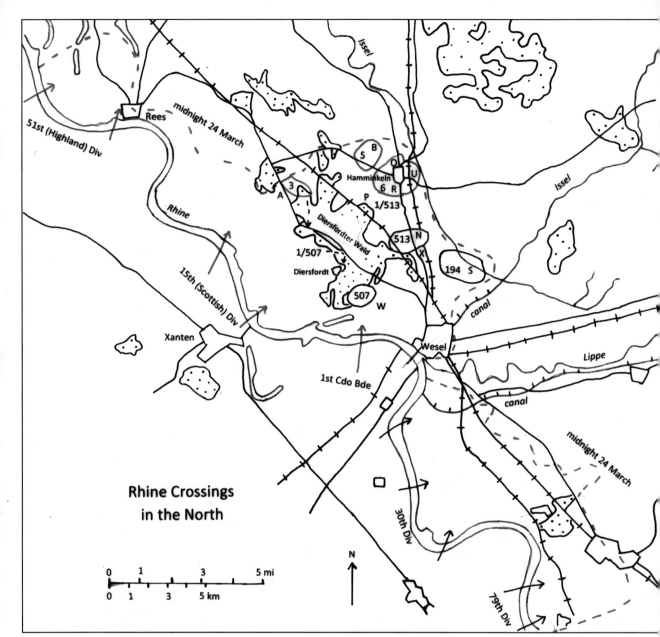

Rhine Crossings in the North (After MacDonald, *The Last Offensive*, map XII).

airfields in northern France. The flights would meet in the skies above Brussels and proceed to Germany. The scale of the effort was indicated by the number of aircraft required for the 17th Airborne. The 507th Parachute Infantry and associated troops rode in 226 C-47 aircraft. An additional 610 C-47s provided tows – at times double tows – for 906 gliders. The 513th Parachute Infantry flew in most of the seventy-two C-46 planes, each carrying a 'double stick' of thirty-six parachutists. The air fleet once assembled required more than two hours to pass over a given point on the ground.[2]

The Allies had gained confidence and some knowledge during their previous airborne efforts. A desire to have as many troops as possible land simultaneously led to a decision to have two gliders towed by a single transport. While one wave was therefore required, the possibility of mid-air entanglements was increased and the gliders would be arriving at unsecured landing zones. Americans still parachuted 75mm pack howitzers into the drop zones and one glider artillery unit transported assembled 105mm howitzers. The large British Hamilcar gliders were even more ambitious, carrying some 25-pounder guns and 'Honey' light reconnaissance tanks into the battle zone.

The C-46s represented another effort to maximize the number of parachutists carried but also entailed hidden risks. Since troopers would jump from opposing rear doors, the density of opening parachutes was twice the normal amount. A more serious condition was the lack of self-sealing fuel tanks on these larger aircraft. Since transport planes flew relatively slowly at low altitudes, anti-aircraft shrapnel might cause fuel leakages into heated engines with the inevitable result of catastrophic fires.

Nearly every unit, whether parachute or glider, saw smoke and haze obscuring the ground, and landing on some planned zones was impossible. Various causes were cited: air corps bombing of Wesel, fighting against troops crossing the river, even speculations of intentional smoke laid down by the Germans. Most did not realize until later that much of the haze derived from Allied smoke generated to provide cover for infantry crossing the Rhine in boats.

The British Over the Rhine

The 6th Airborne would land north of the 17th in zones stretching from the Diersfordter Wald in the west to the vicinity of the small settlement of Hamminkeln near the River Issel in the east. The division was composed of two parachute brigades and an airlanding brigade, each with three battalions. Third Parachute Brigade dropped onto Zone A near Diersfordter Wald and being at the western end was most likely to make contact with British land forces crossing the Rhine. Fifth Parachute Brigade intended to land north and east while 6th Airlanding Brigade arriving in gliders on various landing zones was expected to seize Hamminkeln and six bridges across the Issel.

The British battalions experienced flights lasting about three hours and jumped from their planes close to 10.00am. Those in 3rd Parachute Brigade were on their objectives fairly rapidly but encountered opposition on the drop zone. Transports carrying 1st Canadian Battalion evidently did not slow down or lift their tails – the latter would possibly decrease collisions with parachutists – resulting in dispersion with numerous troopers landing east of the zone. The anti-aircraft flak was considered heavy and several aircraft fell from the sky in flames. Most of the casualties were sustained from ground fire directed on the drop zone; the battalion would suffer sixty-seven casualties (10 per cent) including their commander Lieutenant

Colonel Jeff Nicklin who was killed. Their objectives were nevertheless taken by midday and a defensive position established. One company continued to receive considerable enemy fire but at the same time the quantities of prisoners became an increasing problem. By mid-afternoon a reconnaissance patrol established contact with the 15th Scottish Division that crossed the Rhine earlier in the day.[3]

The 8th Parachute Battalion noticed limited flak crossing the Rhine but anti-aircraft fire increased quickly. By 11.00am the companies had for the most part assembled. Some members of the battalion arrived in Horsa gliders, two of which went missing while another crashed into the woods injuring the commander Lieutenant Colonel G. Hewetson and killing the intelligence officer. By mid-afternoon battalion units reached their objective south of Drop Zone A and later established links with Second Army infantry and American paratroopers. Their casualties numbered 112 or 16 per cent.[4]

Ninth Parachute Battalion saw the flak near the planes of 8th Battalion and some of their aircraft were hit with two catching on fire and one crash-landing with an engine ablaze. Their gliders landed slightly later amid heavier anti-aircraft fire. Most of the battalion assembled just before 11.00am and moved off to objectives in the wooded area south of Drop Zone A. Between midday and mid-afternoon the three companies secured hilltops named 'Dick' and 'Harry' in addition to establishing a position at the south-eastern corner of the woods. A patrol later established contact with the US 1/513th that jumped north of their intended zone.[5]

Fifth Parachute Brigade arrived above their Drop Zone B north-west of the village of Hamminkeln after 10.00am and the three battalions jumped on the zone that remained under enemy artillery fire. The airborne landings followed the ground assault instead of preceding it as in previous operations. The goal was to increase accumulation of troops across the river and impede movement of enemy reinforcements. The brigade would hold opposing ends of the drop zone using the 12th and 13th Battalions while the third – the 7th – would be available to assist troops at either end.

The 7th Parachute Battalion jumped onto the zone at 10.18am, finding the location obscured by smoke. They believed the enemy were caught unawares at first but still managed to place the zone under mortar and artillery fire throughout the morning. The battalion reported ninety-three casualties or 14.6 per cent including a wounded commanding officer, Lieutenant Colonel Geoffrey Pine-Coffin. Two Horsa gliders that each carried a jeep-trailer combination with ammunition did not arrive. A patrol from Company A held the 'Fortnum' crossroads to the west until nearly 9.00pm when the group withdrew as the enemy advanced. The battalion established a position north of the Diersfordter Wald and south-west of Hamminkeln.

Twelfth Battalion undertook their jump amid a considerable amount of anti-aircraft flak and landed to the north-west of the intended area. Enemy shelling of the drop zone caused casualties until the batteries were attacked and subdued. One of the battalion Horsa gliders was hit in flight, while the other landed near the headquarters rendezvous point but was struck by artillery that killed all aboard. Company C seized an objective to the south-west while Companies A and B occupied positions near the rendezvous point on the eastern edge of the zone. By late morning the battalion moved about 600 yards in the direction of Hamminkeln. No counter-attack occurred against their position. Casualties numbered ninety or 14 per cent.

Thirteenth Battalion was carried in thirty-three Dakotas (C-47s) and two Horsa gliders. Most of the casualties were sustained due to anti-aircraft artillery when the battalion landed east of Drop Zone B due to poor visibility. One of the Horsas that carried a mortar section did not arrive. Some delay in organizing the battalion was occasioned by landings east of the zone. During the mid-afternoon an outpost of Company A repulsed an attack. Artillery shelling continued but no additional counter-attacks were launched.[6]

Difficulties associated with glider transport were illustrated by the fate of the glider element of 591st Parachute Squadron Royal Engineers with the 5th Brigade. It should be noted each carried two pilots and four or five sappers and officers:

No. 1: shot up after landing by artillery, one survivor described as 'badly shocked'.
No. 2: all passengers and pilots survived, the jeep and trailer were recovered.
No. 3: the wreckage of this glider held no survivors.
No. 4: nothing was known of this glider at the time the report was written.
No. 5: landed at correct location and was the only group to reach intended objective.
No. 6: artillery and small arms fire after landing killed most occupants; survivors were one pilot, one sapper and Lance Sergeant Fraser who was wounded.

The group from glider No. 5 moved to the road bridge over the River Issel occupied by the 1st Battalion Royal Ulster Rifles since 11.15am. Lieutenant Cox with the 591st Royal Engineers removed the German fire controls but incorporated their explosives on the bridge into the British system. A small 'firing' party remained at the bridge as Cox learned no sappers were present at the road bridge to the north, an objective of the 2nd Oxfordshire and Buckinghamshire Light Infantry. Since the bridge was inaccessible during daylight hours, Lieutenant Cox and a small group completed a hazardous passage to the span after dark, being shelled by both German and British guns. Shortly after 2.00am on 25 March they placed explosive charges on the bridge that was blown up about 3.00am when infantry and armour were heard approaching from the village of Ringenberg to the east.[7]

The third major British infantry formation and one that landed furthest to the east was 6th Airlanding Brigade. The gliders travelled more slowly and arrived somewhat later over the Rhine. The 6th Brigade units took off around 7.00am from various fields. As they approached the target zone, the brigade found that both the river and east bank were obscured by smoke and dust. The gliders cast off about 10.25am amid heavy anti-aircraft fire that caused some gliders to fall from the sky and others to explode.

Glider landings were hampered by poor visibility and the zones were held by enemy troops. One fortunate occurrence was the earlier erroneous landing of various groups from the 513th Parachute Infantry. The British later stated that the assistance of their American cousins saved many casualties on the landing zones among the glider troops.

The 6th Brigade contained three battalions. The 1st Battalion Royal Ulster Rifles seized a road bridge across the River Issel after 11.00am as discussed. Their success had not come without challenges. The commander Lieutenant Colonel Jack Carson was injured in a glider crash and the second in command, Major J. Rickford, did not appear until mid-afternoon. Two armoured cars from the German 116th Panzer Reconnaissance Battalion present on the landing zone were dispatched by a 6-pounder anti-tank gun that landed with the battalion.

The 2nd Battalion Ox and Bucks Light Infantry reported it reached its objectives that included a road bridge across the Issel leading to Ringenberg and possibly the railroad bridge to the north across the river by late morning. The 12th Battalion The Devonshire Regiment indicated it had largely completed occupation of the village of Hamminkeln by 1.00pm.

Control of the bridges provided the brigade with an eastern barrier along the Issel. Artillery and rocket attacks by Typhoon aircraft at various times during the afternoon and evening were directed at the village of Ringenberg and troop concentrations on the east side of the river. Nevertheless, the 2nd Ox Bucks reported an attack directed at its road bridge early on the morning of 25 March that led the 6th Airborne Division to approve destruction of the span.[8]

The 6th Brigade later described the glider landings to be 'very satisfactory' due in large measure to the highly-skilled pilots. The German light flak guns took a heavy toll and the brigade thought in future operations the drop and landing zones should be pounded by fighter-bombers and Typhoon rockets for at least half an hour before landings. The 12th Devons added comments to the brigade report noting that heavy loads such as guns and tanks came in too early. The assistance of the American paratroopers and Typhoon aircraft in overcoming resistance on the landing zones and as a consequence preventing greater casualties was readily acknowledged.[9]

Casualties among the 6th Brigade were initially considered heavy. The 1st RUR sustained losses of 32 per cent, or 16 officers and 243 soldiers among the 810 who landed on the first day. The 2nd Ox Bucks estimated losses around 50 per cent of the 850 who landed; during mid-afternoon they reported roughly 400 casualties due to landing mishaps or enemy action. The 12th Devons fared better, reporting 140 casualties including 81 missing, or 16.7 per cent of the 840 present. These initial estimates may have been modified once accountings of the missing were completed.

The Americans in 17th Airborne Division

The 1st Battalion of the 507th Parachute Infantry jumped shortly before 10.00am and landed in a field beyond the town of Diersfordt, a location well to the north and west of the intended Drop Zone W. The regimental commander, Colonel Edson Raff, led a group north-east that cleared out German infantry and ultimately subdued a battery of 150mm artillery pieces. They headed for a fortified manor known as 'Diersfordt Castle' encountering another group from the battalion. An attack was launched on the castle. As Company A advanced the 3rd Battalion from the 507th arrived to assume responsibility for subduing the garrison. Leaving their company already involved in the attack, 1/507th moved to the assigned location by 2.00pm.

The 2nd and 3rd Battalions both landed on Drop Zone W where the resistance was heaviest along the northern and eastern edges. 3/507th proceeded north-west to Diersfordt to assume the role of reducing the castle on a room by room basis. A final stand of resistance by officers was overcome. The battalion reported 500 prisoners captured and five tanks destroyed, two by a new weapon, the 57mm recoilless rifle. 2/507th assembled quickly and moved west and south-west to their objectives with positions consolidated by 11.00am. In the early afternoon Company F established contact with British infantry that crossed earlier in the day.

The 464th Parachute Field Artillery also landed on Drop Zone W shortly after 10.00am. Their machine guns provided covering fire as they began to retrieve bundles containing portions of their 75mm pack artillery. By noon four howitzers were firing from a position about 1,500 yards north-east of the drop zone with an additional five in action an hour later. The artillery battalion carried twelve pieces and bundles; one bundle may have been accidently dropped en route, some sustained damage in the drop. A tenth howitzer was assembled from the surviving parts.

By the end of the day, the 507th Parachute Infantry established contact with elements of the 6th Airborne Division in the north and the 1st Commando in the south. Casualties sustained represented about 7 per cent of the regiment.[10]

The 513th Parachute Infantry landed around 10.00am but did so roughly 2500 yards north-west of their intended drop zone. Since the actual landing areas overlapped into the British zones, many of the parachute infantry provided substantial assistance to the glider troops by helping to clear contested locations. The 1st Battalion encountered heavy resistance in its drop zone and several commanding officers were not present at the outset. Those assembled forces moved south about 500 yards. Other units joined, enabling the battalion to form a defensive perimeter. Shortly after midday various officers arrived including Colonel James Coutts who commanded the regiment. Another advance began around 1.30pm, in this instance to the south-east to their assigned position as regimental reserve.

The 2nd Battalion also landed in an area covered by German small arms fire. The jump must still have been fairly tight as they reported assembly within less than one hour. After clearing their drop area, movement to the south-east was undertaken but it proved necessary to overcome or bypass locations of enemy resistance. Once they reached their intended assembly area and realized it had been cleared, the battalion companies moved through comparatively light resistance to their objective along the wooded area east of Diersfordt. The 1/507th had cleared the objective so the battalion occupied a position in the vicinity.

The 3rd Battalion of the 513th assembled in three separate groups following the jump. Two groups initially moved north-east before realizing they landed at the wrong location. These soldiers reversed course to the south-east and arrived during the afternoon to find the third group already present. The northern assembly area was cleared, then the objective was secured by about 4.30pm. Contact was established with 194th Glider Infantry to the south and elements of 6th Airborne about half an hour later.

The 466th Parachute Field Artillery actually landed on the correct Drop Zone X to find the location under fire. Opposition was subdued and some howitzers were assembled quickly but during the process all the officers in one battery were killed or wounded. The battalion reached its planned area of operation by midday and all thirteen pack howitzers were present by 3.00pm.[11]

The 194th Glider Infantry and 681st Glider Field Artillery arrived in gliders from double tows about 10.30am and despite visual challenges arising from smoke and dust many set down on the correct Landing Zone S north of Wesel and near canal bridges. The 1st Battalion assembled rapidly and moved north-west with Company A to the east and Company C to the west. They passed through areas on which other gliders landed and most reached objectives by 2.00pm, although Company C was delayed by enemy resistance.

The 2nd Battalion reputedly placed many gliders on the intended location while some landed east of the River Issel canal. (However, the battalion report offered a different assessment as indicated below.) A sufficient number assembled within less than one hour to begin movement towards their objective. The reserve Company E entered the assembly area shortly after midday. During the course of the day the battalion withstood four counter-attacks.

The 3rd Battalion encountered both anti-aircraft and small arms fire while landing that resulted in casualties. They reached their reserve position later in the afternoon and extended patrols west to the 507th, north to the 3/513th and encountered the British 1st Commando Brigade to the south. The 194th Glider Infantry sustained 444 casualties or 16 per cent during the operation.

Their supporting 75mm howitzers derived from the 681st Glider Field Artillery Battalion that landed with them. The various batteries opposed enemy forces as they assembled on the landing zone then moved to their intended firing positions. One unit – Battery A – received calls for support en route and established impromptu firing positions until 2.00pm when they continued onward. By later in the afternoon ten of the twelve howitzers were firing. Communications were established with both divisional artillery and regimental commands and by using radio with artillery on the west bank of the Rhine earlier in the afternoon.

The 680th Glider Field Artillery brought in heavier 105mm howitzers with 50 per cent setting down on the correct landing zone around 11.40am. Enemy artillery fire destroyed numerous gliders after landing. After midday six pieces were ready to fire and by 5.00pm nine howitzers were placed in position with 900 rounds stockpiled.

Various factors such as smoke and anti-aircraft fire that shot down some tow planes resulted in 2/194th landings about 1500 yards north and 500 yards west of the intended zone. Some gliders arrived with wounded aboard. Landing fields were generally small and gliders collided with fences but few injuries resulted. However, the battalion set down within range of enemy artillery that fired on and set some gliders ablaze. As the quantity of troops increased enemy positions were overcome. The battalion commander Lieutenant Colonel Stewart was an early casualty and command was assumed by Major Pleasant Martin. Company F managed to overcome enemy resistance centred on a farm selected as regimental headquarters during planning. The farm was evidently a favoured location as a German regimental command was in residence at the time of the landings.

Companies F and G made progress as Company E devoted attention to pockets of enemy resistance bypassed during the advance. After midday a counter-attack by two tanks was halted by anti-tank guns and one tank was destroyed by a bazooka round. By early afternoon Company F reached its objective and began to establish a defensive position. Shortly afterwards contact was established with 1/194th on the left flank to the north. The battalion and indeed the regiment were positioned within a V formed by the River Issel to the east and the Wesel canal to the south,

All objectives except bridge No. 1 across the Wesel canal had been attained by mid-afternoon. A patrol led by Lieutenant Wittig attempted to move along the north side of the canal to reach the bridge but was halted by enemy fire. A group from Company E under Lieutenant Robinson moved at dusk to locate Wittig but found only one dead soldier from the platoon.

During darkness the battalion became concerned about the security of its west flank with reports of possible infiltrations. A heavy artillery barrage struck about midnight as contact with Company G was lost and heavy small arms fire was heard in the area of that unit. A patrol from Company E made a disconcerting discovery about

2.00am. German infantry and one armoured vehicle were located in the rear area behind the Company G location, considered an indication their position had been overrun. One officer, Lieutenant Anderson, had studied maps and sand tables of the terrain and was able to call down an effective barrage from Corps artillery.

Shortly afterwards Company F sustained an attack from several tanks and infantry that was halted by fire from both artillery and rifle positions. Indications of assembly for another attack were heard when a patrol reported that the Company G location had been overrun and a gap existed on its flank with Company F. Personnel from the headquarters in the rear of Company G came forward to halt a German attempt to exploit the gap.

By 5.00am firing eased along the front and at dawn about 6.00am a runner arrived from Company G to state that despite heavy casualties, particularly on the left at the gap, two platoons were holding their positions. The company would shortly move forward in attack. A dawn patrol under Lieutenant Robinson finally reached the last bridge, No. 1. Just before 7.00am Lieutenant Witting and eight men from his platoon arrived having entered Wesel the previous evening where contact with the British 1st Commando was established.[12]

Memories

James Gavin for once had the opportunity to view an airborne operation as an observer from an aircraft not participating in the jump:

> Yesterday took off at 0815 … over Venlo at 0955 there we sighted the US 17th and British 6th on their way into Opn Varsity. Quite a sight, as far as the eye could see wave upon wave of planes, fighters darting about. And ahead billowing clouds of dust and smoke from the battle area. They appeared to hit their DZs a bit early, the flak initially was heavy in both sectors, the americans were on the right and the British left. As the dropping progressed the US flak stopped but the british continued quite heavily finally throwing up bursts after the last landing made. Counted over a dozen ships shot down, the C-47s get in trouble with their poor gas tanks [possibly referring to C46s without self-sealing tanks]. In some cases the crews bailed out in most they went down in a ball of fire. Crossed over into the german sector to get a close up view of the DZ area and was fired at by small arms fire. Was down to about 1,000ft at the time. We had been observing at 2,500. The US TCC formations were beautiful, the british not as tight, bomber stream in fact, and they flew finally at 3,000ft. The DZ patterns did not look too bad, at least some of them were excellent. But all in all it was a very rough show and, in fact, it appeared a bit dangerous.[13]

When Irv Hennings of Company A/513th jumped from the C-46 aircraft his parachute did not fully open. Since there were so many open parachutes nearby he 'rode lightly' on the one below without collapsing that chute. The ground below him had been ploughed in anticipation of spring planting. He still landed hard in the field and was rendered unconscious. He regained consciousness and tried to find his unit but had to backtrack since he was fired upon from nearby farms before finding the company.

Herb Anderson in command of Company A described the air as black with anti-aircraft bursts. While descending he saw men being shot from the ground so slipped his parachute sideways closer to a row of trees. A German position containing four soldiers with rifles and a machine gun was visible. He experienced a hard landing only about 100ft away from the position, injuring ligaments in his leg. The four young soldiers with rifles surrendered but the position also held a Private Schmidt wounded during the jump. Captain Anderson applied a tourniquet, a process rendered difficult since the wound was near the top of Schmidt's leg, and administered a morphine syrette. He came to a house and commandeered a bicycle that by the end of the day he exchanged for a horse. During the evening Herb visited the regimental aid post that recommended surgery for his leg. At first he declined but agreed once he could not reinsert his foot in the boot. He left command of the company once his leg was placed in a cast.

Private First Class John Kormann from the 517th Signal Company was of German descent and received a letter from his mother just before the operation asking him to show mercy if an opportunity arose. Although trained as a parachutist, he was disappointed to learn he had been assigned to a glider containing a jeep and four soldiers with a pilot and co-pilot as crew. They were fed a pre-flight breakfast of steak and eggs, which probably indicated they might be up against it.

The tow plane pulled two gliders. Shortly after take-off the glider stream passed over Notre-Dame cathedral in Chartres. He subsequently saw a French farmer peacefully ploughing fields, a scene completely at variance with his own near future. Private Kormann's glider crashed 'right over a German artillery battery. We slid along, bashed into a tree and came to rest with the jeep pointing straight up. I remember being half-conscious but at least we survived.' Vivid memories included seeing a dead glider pilot nearby and witnessing a fellow fall from a B-24 bomber dropping supplies over the landing zone.

Infantry from 3/513th crossed a nearby field and Major Anderson sent a group over to clear some houses about 250 yards away. John was passing the last house with a slanted door to the cellar when he heard noises. He pulled the pin from a grenade and called out in German for the occupants to surrender. Receiving no response, he again called out and more than a dozen women, children and old men climbed from the cellar. They helped him find the pin to insert in the grenade handle. His 'mother's mercy' saved their lives and spared him a lifetime of regret.[14]

The Wounded

Since relief was a broad river away, medical treatment was undertaken by units that either parachuted in or landed by glider until evacuation could begin on D+1, 25 March. During 24 March the 195th Airlanding unit arriving with British glider troops established a casualty collecting point by noon on the outskirts of Hamminkeln. Two advanced dressing stations opened south and east of the town and by 4.00pm the main dressing station was located on Landing Zone U near the River Issel bridge seized by the 1st RUR. A steady flow of casualties arrived with 333 admissions on the 24th. Nine operations were undertaken and at the end of the day 329 patients remained since four had died.

The 225th Field Ambulance unit landed in gliders with the battalions and headquarters of 5th Parachute Brigade. Captain G.S. Shiell was killed on the drop zone. Their main dressing station with two operating theatres was in place near DZ B by midday and senior medical officers appeared during the afternoon as casualties arrived from the regimental aid post. When evacuations began on 25 March the station held 310 wounded. Twenty-six major surgical procedures were undertaken in the first two days.

The sister medical unit with the 3rd Parachute, the 224th, established their main dressing station by mid-afternoon, addressing nine major surgical cases by midnight and an additional nineteen the next day. The unit conducted sixty-eight surgeries from landing through the end of March, with 460 patients arriving during that period. Most injuries were gunshot wounds with mortar or shell shrapnel wounds decreasing as the week-long period progressed.

Wounds and injuries requiring surgery were categorized as consisting of thirty-three compound fractures (fourteen of the femur), five traumatic amputations, seven abdominal and twenty-three other wounds. Nine of the surgical patients – five Germans and four British – died, representing only 2 per cent of the overall admissions. Intermittent evacuations began on the 25th but before that time surgeons rarely had time for post-operative checks.

The 224th employed penicillin both as an injection and in local applications but had not been able to evaluate results. As had been observed in Normandy, the importance of whole blood could not be overstated. Blood had not been available until D+1 and thereafter in limited quantities. The unit noted that the most seriously wounded – those who would not survive a trip to any but the most forward of medical stations – had to have whole blood rather than plasma.

The American 224th Airborne Medical Company landed on Landing Zone N south-east of Hamminkeln at midday. Since the area had not been cleared, medical personnel and glider pilots were wounded by enemy fire. The company assembled and moved to the south-west where a casualty clearing station was established in the general area occupied by the 1/513th Parachute Infantry. By the close of the first day

394 soldiers had arrived, among them 117 seriously wounded, 175 slightly wounded and thirty-three injured. Twenty-three surgical procedures addressed seven sucking wounds, eight compound fractures and eight cases of wounds either to abdominal or maxillo-facial regions. Evacuations did not begin until the following morning when ambulances began to arrive. During that day an additional 270 cases arrived including fifty-three serious and 163 lighter wounds, twenty-one injured and two instances of disease.[15]

Evaluation

An accounting for Varsity is somewhat elusive. The 6th Airborne sustained losses of 19.4 per cent among the 7,220 troops who landed. In addition, about a quarter of the British glider pilots were casualties. The 17th Airborne percentage was lower: 13.5 per cent of the 9,650 troops involved.[16]

More than fifty gliders and forty-four transport planes were destroyed and another 332 damaged. Impacts during and after jumps were especially severe to planes carrying 5th Parachute Brigade (52 per cent of 121 Dakotas including sixteen destroyed) and 513th Parachute Infantry (70 per cent of 114 planes, with twenty-one of them destroyed). The US IX Troop Carrier Command listed air crew losses of forty-one killed, 153 wounded and 163 missing. After the landings occurred, 240 B-24 Liberator bombers from US Eighth Air Force flew at low levels to resupply the landing zones and fifteen or sixteen did not return.[17]

Casualties in 17th Airborne on 24 March included 159 killed, 522 wounded and 240 missing. On the same day the 30th and 79th Infantry Divisions lost forty-one killed, 450 wounded and seven missing crossing the Rhine south of Wesel and in subsequent fighting.[18]

The objectives of Operation Varsity were achieved and included the virtual destruction of the German 84th Division and isolation of a portion of that division, 1053rd Infantry, in an area north of Diersfordt. However, MacDonald argued the landings were likely unnecessary especially given the costs in men and machines and the close proximity of the objectives to the Rhine crossing locations.[19] Perhaps this was another instance of pressure to use this new force of specially trained soldiers in a role closer to that employed in Normandy.

In the end the 17th Airborne and 6th Airborne soldiers would come to feel their efforts were submerged and forgotten within the more general Allied crossing of the Rhine in the north. Varsity was the last airborne operation of such substantial size during the war and given the advent of guided missiles and jet propulsion will not be repeated.

Forney photographed soldiers from the 517th Airborne Signal Company boarding a glider in the pre-dawn darkness. John Kormann belonged to this company that left from a field near Chartres, possibly the one near Coulmiers. (*NARA*)

Troops aboard a glider before take-off, as photographed by Forney. (*NARA*)

Arnowitz recorded an image of troops marching to gliders on the morning of Varsity at Field A-50 near Orléans, possibly near Coulmiers. (*NARA*)

Troopers from the 513th Parachute Infantry arriving at their transports, with a row of C-46 aircraft marked Z7 in the background. Forney was the photographer. The C-46 carried twice the number of parachutists but had not been fitted with self-sealing fuel tanks in contrast to many C-47 aircraft. (NARA)

A photograph taken by Harris showing members of the 513th boarding a C-46 craft including a group with 'Apache' haircuts. *(NARA)*

(**Above**) Forney observed a group of parachutists boarding a transport, probably a C-46. (*NARA*)

(**Opposite, above**) In a photograph taken by Harris, members of the 513th boarding a C-46 craft marked Z7. (*NARA*)

(**Opposite, below**) Heimberger recorded an image of a C-47 marked L4 with double glider tows on a runway. (*NARA*)

(**Above**) Arnowitz observed transports and gliders beginning to fill the sky above Field A-50. (*NARA*)

(**Opposite, above**) One of the C-46 transports, marked H2, crashed on take-off but fortunately did not burn. Harris recorded the aftermath. (*NARA*)

(**Opposite, below**) The photographer Clyde Pletcher exposed an image of double towed gliders from the cockpit of a neighbouring aircraft. (*NARA*)

203397

(**Above**) Mayhew photographed a nearby C-47 in the air towing two gliders (*NARA*)

(**Opposite, above**) The photographer Quant exposed images of paratroopers jumping from planes before the B-17 in which he was flying was shot down. Quant managed to successfully bail out with his exposed film but some of negatives were damaged. The journalist Richard C. Hottelet ('Big Jump into Germany') was another passenger who jumped to safety. (*NARA*)

(**Opposite, below**) Parachutes were opening below transport aircraft in another of the photographs from the doomed B-17. The pilot managed to crash land the plane in a field but one of the passengers who jumped did not survive. (*NARA*)

The transport planes appear to be C-47s so the units jumping were probably members of the 507th Parachute Infantry in another Quant image. (*NARA*)

Eisenhower watched the landings on the opposite side of the Rhine. (*NARA*)

Troopers jumping from the double doors on opposite sides of the C-46 that resulted in unusually dense concentrations of parachutes in the air. (NARA)

Troopers after landing with a glider in the background. Small fields and fences made for challenging landings. (NARA)

(**Opposite, above**) McCleery landed with the 17th Airborne commander Major General William Miley (second from left) and his staff. (*NARA*)

(**Opposite, below**) McCleery subsequently observed troops hugging the ground as small arms fire passed overhead. (*NARA*)

(**Above**) Some of the 17th Airborne troops advancing after landing. (*NARA*)

(**Above**) McCleery glanced upward to photograph a damaged transport plane with its starboard wing on fire. (*NARA*)

(**Opposite, above**) A group of 'Raff's Ruffians' peering into the woods near their landing area, possibly the 1/507th that dropped well north of their intended zone. (*NARA*)

(**Opposite, below**) A group from the 507th described as 'Raff's Ruffians' moved out following landing. The regimental commander was Colonel Edson Raff. (*NARA*)

203236

(**Opposite, above**) Pletcher noticed troopers, evidently from the 513th, close to the ground with a large British Hamilcar glider in the background. (*NARA*)

(**Opposite, below**) The British Hamilcar glider served to transport heavy loads. Pletcher photographed the craft that may have been the same one shown in the previous image. (*NARA*)

(**Above**) Pletcher waited with a group of infantry behind jeeps following landings west of the Rhine. (*NARA*)

Pletcher recorded a member of the 513th crouching behind a jeep while a paratrooper from the 6th British Airborne stood nearby. Mixture of units occurred when Americans from the 513th landed north in the British area. This happy coincidence provided help in clearing the British zones. (*NARA*)

Pletcher noted the unloading of a jeep from glider 42. (NARA)

Pletcher observed soldiers who commandeered a wagon and team of horses. *(NARA)*

Troops near the wagon were getting organized following the jump. *(NARA)*

Pletcher encountered one unfortunate glider landing that resulted in a scattering of supply canisters. (*NARA*)

Pletcher photographed a line of German prisoners held by the 513th Parachute Infantry. (*NARA*)

One of the soldiers lost in the operation, probably from the 513th, was observed by Pletcher hanging from his parachute in a tree. *(NARA)*

A more general scene revealed this or another paratrooper hanging near an encampment. (NARA)

Pearson recorded B-24 bombers crossing the Rhine at low altitudes on supply missions. These planes were therefore vulnerable to anti-aircraft fire. (NARA)

(**Opposite, above**) McCleery recorded a classic portrait of an injured paratrooper who was still ready for a fight. (*NARA*)

(**Above**) Corrado observed a gathering of Allied commanders on 25 March across the Rhine at Lintfort. British Field Marshals Montgomery and Alanbrooke spoke with American Generals Bradley and William Simpson, whose Ninth Army served under British command. (*NARA*)

(**Opposite, below**) Winston Churchill stood on the 25th with American General Charles Brown of XVI Corps. The Prime Minister's careless behavior during the previous day led some to wonder if he hoped to die on this battlefield. (*NARA*)

A picnic was held at Lintfort on the east bank of the Rhine on the 25th. Chicken and spirits were on the menu and it was the latter the censor sought to conceal. The conversation was later remembered very differently. Eisenhower stated (*Crusade in Europe*, 372) that Alanbrooke now understood and completely agreed with the strategic approach. Alanbrooke subsequently was mystified by this statement since he contended Ike's strategy had been entirely wrong (Bryant, *Triumph in the West*, 343). (*NARA*)

Hard fighting remained for the 30th Infantry that crossed the Rhine in boats on the previous day. Tesser photographed a portion of the division advancing under fire against enemy opposition on the 25th. (*NARA*)

The 30th Division encountered armoured vehicles and was slowed in their advance by the presence of a German half-track damaged or destroyed on the road. *(NARA)*

Chapter Five

The Allies in Germany

Unexpected events awaited the troops during their advance into the Reich. They were surprised at the reactions of many civilians and astounded by some of the works of art encountered. They were disgusted by the brutality meted out to fellow human beings on an unimaginable scale. The Americans lost their president in April and during the second week of May received news of a most welcome nature.

* * *

Beyond the Rhine

Once the British Second Army and American Ninth Army crossed the Rhine near Wesel major advances carried them eastward into northern Germany and southward to the industrial centres of the Ruhr. The Ninth Army returned to Bradley's command at 12th Army Group and encircled the district from the north as First Army moved up from the south. Once the forces joined on 1 April, the fate of German Army Group B – whose divisions and armies opposed the Allies from Normandy onward – was at last sealed. Resistance continued for three weeks but this time the pocket would not be opened from the outside. More than 300,000 German soldiers surrendered in the Ruhr by late April. Their commander, Field Marshal Walter Model, chose suicide rather than join them.

Ninth Army began a movement eastward, passing for the most part north of the Harz Mountains. Second Armoured Division reached Magdeburg on the River Elbe by 11 April. A small bridgehead across the Elbe near Magdeburg came under attack by elements of a division in the hastily formed German 12th Army. The limited number of troops from 3/119th Infantry in 30th Division and the 41st Armoured Infantry in the 2nd Armoured Division had virtually no anti-tank defences and were for a time isolated on 13–14 April. Some of these troops were captured and others withdrew to the west bank. Another bridgehead further to the south rendered the abandoned bridgehead of limited value. The effort represented a rare success for German arms that month.

Given their position roughly 70 miles from Berlin, Ninth Army believed they would be released to drive onward to the German capital. However, Bradley informed

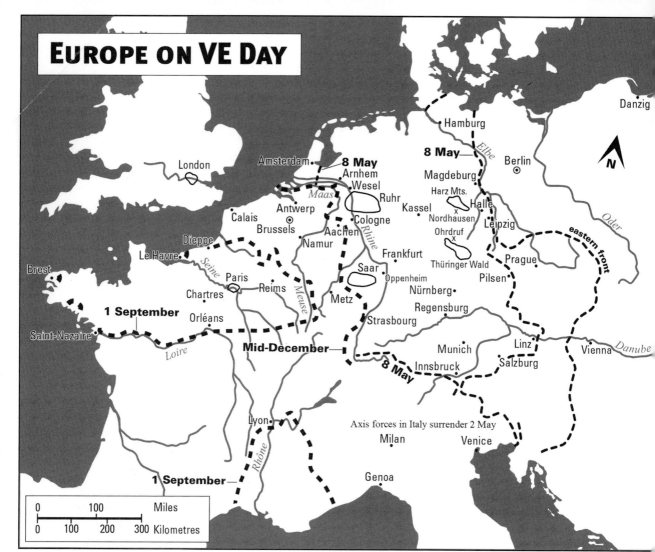

Europe on VE Day.

William Simpson who commanded that army that they would not advance in any strength beyond the Elbe. Eisenhower was under considerable pressure from Prime Minister Churchill and the British chiefs of staff to recognize future political ramifications to justify movement to the east. Ike consulted with Bradley concerning the projected numbers of casualties required to capture Berlin; Bradley responded perhaps 100,000. Both generals thought it unnecessary to advance eastward only to subsequently fall back to boundaries agreed upon previously with the Russians.[1]

First Army reached positions on the River Mulde that flowed northward into the Elbe between Leipzig and Magdeburg. In the process army troops including the 1st Infantry Division moved through the Harz Mountains where the German 11th Army was overcome and 12th Army – created in the forlorn hope of relieving encircled troops in the Ruhr – had organized. The latter army would instead be called north-east in a woefully insufficient effort to disperse Russian forces near Berlin. The movement of First Army to the Mulde was accomplished after encountering some fierce resistance among the ring of anti-aircraft defences west of Halle. The defences were intended to protect vital war industries producing synthetic rubber, petroleum and hydrogen among other materials. A combat command from 9th Armoured Division finally bypassed the southern end of the defences to arrive at the Mulde on 15 April and cross the following day. The 2nd Infantry Division continued with efforts to reduce the defences of Leipzig some miles west of the Elbe, including a bizarre stand by a determined group in the stone base of a monument erected to celebrate Napoleon's 1813 defeat at the Battle of Nations.

Eventually 69th Division troops from First Army would cross the Mulde and encounter Russian forces at the town of Torgau near the Elbe on 25 April. Early that day other patrols met Russians at nearby locations on the Elbe, but Torgau became enshrined in legend as the first meeting in the field between Eastern and Western Allies.[2]

The 5th Division in Third Army completed clearance of the city of Frankfurt on 25 March as intensity of fighting lessened and opposition reduced to municipal service members including firemen and police supporting the few remaining troops. During the period 28 to 30 March the 6th Armoured Division in XX Corps moved 100 miles north-east to the vicinity of Kassel, where resistance proved so heavy the 80th Infantry Division devoted three days to overcoming German defenders. This movement occurred east of the efforts by First and Ninth Armies to encircle the Ruhr.

The 4th and 11th Armoured Divisions in XII Corps moved eastward in attacks during early April, with both crossing the River Werra on 2 April. Bayreuth was seized by 11th Armoured on 14 April following receipt of orders from SHAEF via 12th Army Group that the army would halt at a line from Bayreuth to the River Mulde. On 17 April renewed attacks drove to the south-east and troops would proceed south along the border of Czechoslovakia. By 21 April movement extended towards Austria with the intention of meeting Russian forces in the vicinity of Linz.

The 4th Armoured transferred to VIII Corps in the centre of the army area and pushed on to the town of Gotha where a command and control centre was reported. The centre was found on 4 April. A gruesome discovery was encountered that day at the Lager near Ohrdruf. Patton was so appalled he contacted Omar Bradley to insist both he and Eisenhower see the horrors themselves, which they did on 12 April. On 17 April divisions in VIII Corps reached the 'restraining line' established by SHAEF and 12th Army Group.

American armoured divisions in the three corps of Third Army moved so quickly in early April it proved necessary to hold positions as following infantry divisions completed eradication of bypassed defensive positions before proceeding. During the month from crossing the Rhine in late March to arriving at the various stop lines by the third week in April, Third Army lost 1,757 men killed, 5,885 wounded and 782 missing in action. German losses were estimated to be considerably greater and included surrender of more than 204,000 soldiers.[3]

The final campaign of the war in Europe for Third Army involved crossing the River Danube and entering western portions of Czechoslovakia and Austria. German resistance had in essence crumbled so fighting was limited and numbers of prisoners soared. An overt goal of both Third and the adjacent Seventh Army in their movements southward was to deny German access to the supposed mountainous 'redoubt' that had been a concern raised by Allied intelligence.

The suspected 'National Redoubt' in which leaders of the Third Reich would be defended by fanatical Waffen-SS and other troops became an increasing concern among Allied intelligence circles as it became apparent the German military structure was collapsing. Enigma data decoded from German messages in April revealed some mention of a fortress in the southern mountains and further indicated the German high command would divide into two groups – one in the north near Wismar and another in the south near Salzburg and Berchtesgaden. This bifurcation of the command structure occurred since it seemed likely that communication and ground transportation links to Berlin would be disrupted. In the end Hitler decided to remain in Berlin, and the Allies would later learn that an alpine redoubt essentially existed only in the imaginations of some Nazi officials and Wehrmacht commanders. Nevertheless, Bennett concluded Eisenhower and his intelligence chief Kenneth Strong did not wish to take chances following the failure to discover plans for the Ardennes offensive.[4]

Final efforts by Third Army towards Salzburg and the Danube Valley were initiated on 22 April with movement of troops on the following day from south of Nürnberg. A subsequent boundary shift meant the classical music mecca Salzburg and alpine sports towns including Kitzbühel would fall to Seventh Army. Troops in XX Corps reached the Danube on 25 April and established bridgeheads. Regensburg was entered by 65th Infantry Division two days later. The River Inn on the Austrian border was a goal achieved on 2 May. The 65th Division captured the city of Linz with its Skoda vehicle works on 5 May.

As this final campaign began in late April, XII Corps was positioned on the Czech border but was ordered to patrol along that border rather than cross into the country. Such restrictions must have proved particularly galling: as Patton explained to Bradley, anticipation of authorized fraternization with women from Czechoslovakia, an Allied nation, was a strong motivation in Third Army. On 5 May, 4th Armoured Division did enter the country but received orders to stop.

V Corps transferred from First to Third Army on 3 May. Divisions in the corps included some whose actions in Europe were legendary: 1st, 2nd and 97th Infantry and 9th Armoured Divisions. The corps attacked the following day and entered the Czech city of Pilsen and its industrial district on 6 May. A line east of Pilsen was secured and held as the war in Europe ended on 8 May. During the final campaign, losses in Third Army were 345 killed, 2,069 wounded and 809 missing. German casualties were of course much greater, including more than 412,000 who became prisoners.[5]

The Camps

Anyone who visited a labour or extermination camp – the distinction for many is irrelevant – could not forget the experience. Rumours of concentration camps circulated in Germany[6] and occupied Europe during the war. The Russians revealed the discovery of Treblinka in Poland in the summer of 1944. The magnitude of the crime was its best defence – the stories seemed too horrific to be true.

In April the Western Allies began to encounter such camps in central Germany. Chet Hansen would journey on 12 April to meet Eisenhower, Bradley and Patton at the Ohrdruf Lager near Gotha and the salt mine storage area in Merkers. On this day they passed German civilians on the roads moving furniture, filling bomb craters, rebuilding homes, in essence beginning to recover from the destruction of war even as the war continued. He noticed children waving to trucks filled with American engineers who ignored them. Amidst the military traffic on the autobahn was an old car driven by Frenchmen with their *tricolore* flag on the front and 'two pretty French nurses inside'.

The presence of an estimated 3,200 corpses lying on the ground was only one of the horrors encountered at Ohrdruf. Eisenhower was stunned but not speechless: 'I can't understand the bestiality of those German people that would compel them to do anything like that. Our soldiers could never mutilate bodies the way they have.' Upon learning the Ohrdruf mayor and his wife committed suicide after visiting the Lager, Ike thought their actions 'the most encouraging thing I have heard of. It may indicate that they still have some sensitivities left.'[7]

Eisenhower wisely provided for documentation from the first moments of discovery and some of the most prominent journalists in Europe responded with visits to Dachau and Buchenwald. Edward Murrow closed his chilling radio broadcast with the simple request that the listeners believe what he described had occurred and was still occurring.[8]

Memories in Germany

Irv Hennings commented that most soldiers he knew seemed surprised in Germany. He felt the citizens were very supportive of soldiers, having been militarized since the mid to later 1930s. In addition, civilians knew bombing would stop once the Allied soldiers arrived. Irv was sitting in a café with a gun hanging from his chair when local residents came in asking soldiers to stay in their homes for fear of freed prisoners from slave labour camps. He thought they preferred occupation by Americans or British soldiers. Irv believed civilians did not particularly welcome the French and were afraid of the Russians.

John Kormann spoke German and transferred to the Counter-Intelligence Corps or CIC. His rank was unclear although he had the 'power to arrest' that extended to American officers if necessary. One of CIC's first missions was to cross territory still under German control to arrest a man named Müller for crimes against Allied prisoners. Upon entering the town in a jeep, the team simply asked a passing resident for the address of the person in question. When Müller – described by Kormann as 'a pig-eyed so-and-so' – saw the Americans he bolted for the rear door in an unsuccessful attempt to evade arrest. It was a scene repeated many times across Germany that spring.[9]

The same day of the visit to Ohrdruf Patton led Eisenhower and Bradley to the salt mine storage for artistic works and gold deposits found by 90th Division troops a few days earlier. The three generals had supper in the former barracks adjacent to Patton's caravan then talked well into the night. Eisenhower evidently revealed his thoughts that the Western Allies would not seek to move beyond the River Elbe to occupy Berlin. Patton returned to his sleeping quarters in the caravan only to learn from a radio broadcast that President Roosevelt had died. He returned to the barracks to inform Bradley and Eisenhower.

Hansen found himself in a jeep on 13 April as Bradley toured Hessen Nassau in the Ruhr area with First Army commander Courtney Hodges. They passed traces of recent battles: smoke rising from burned wooden buildings and villagers burying their dead residents. The extent to which Germany promoted decentralized industry in response to Allied bombing was evident. Small manufacturing or fabricating concerns were found with a 'concentration camp' for labour adjacent to each industrial village.

Residents and former inmates from these and other camps wandered streets, groups described by Hansen as composed of Russian girls, cocky yet puzzled Italians, and truckloads of former French prisoners driving westward. Thousands both inside and outside camps either had or soon would have freedom but were in the position of 'not knowing what to do with it now that it had come'. He thought German residents had no love for the Americans, being frightened and at the same time unable to comprehend defeat. A Polish major argued for harsh suppression of returning German prisoners of war to prevent any tendencies to resort to guerilla warfare.[10]

(**Opposite, above**) Members of 54th Signal Battalion attached to the 17th Airborne sheltering in a ditch for protection from mortar fire in a photograph by Pletcher on 28 March. (*NARA*)

(**Opposite, below**) The same day Pletcher witnessed soldiers in the 194th Glider Infantry seeking to flush snipers from hiding. Machine gun fire directed against the snipers ignited a haystack. (*NARA*)

(**Right**) Hawkins observed a medic from the 17th Airborne attending to a wounded German on 29 March. The location 'Aetsohembeck' was probably near Münster. (*NARA*)

(**Below**) Troops from the 513th Parachute Infantry received support from the British 6th Guards Armoured Brigade as they entered Münster. The photographer Dwight Miller was present on 2 April. (*NARA*)

(**Opposite, above**) Miller observed the 513th waiting to advance with the 4th Armoured Battalion Coldstream Guards near Münster on 2 April. (*NARA*)

(**Opposite, below**) Pletcher photographed columns of soldiers from the 194th Glider Infantry along a road near Münster on 4 April. (*NARA*)

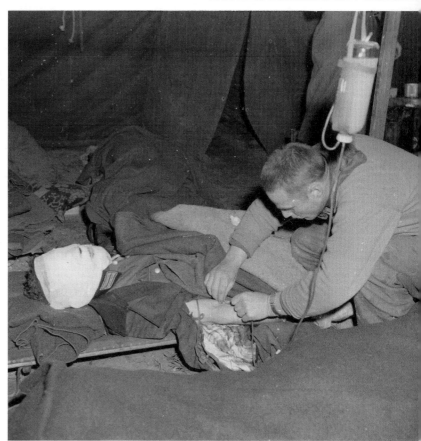

Third Army infantry in the 90th Division discovered a salt mine in Merkers holding stolen art works, German gold bullion, and various looted items such as cigarette cases and gold fillings extracted from teeth. The photographer Lieutenant Leo Moore was present when Eisenhower and Bradley visited the subterranean storage areas with Patton on 12 April. Patton was unimpressed with the 'art' he saw, declaring it of a type generally encountered in American bars (*War As I Knew It*, 275–6). The general was mistaken. The vast underground vaults held antiquities from Egypt, Greece and Rome in addition to more recent works such as Dürer woodcuts and paintings by Cranach, Goya and Rubens (Edsel and Witter, *Monuments Men*, 289–90). (*NARA*)

Ohrdruf Lager or labour camp near the towns of Ohrdruf and Gotha in Thuringia was liberated by 4th Armoured Division in early April. Patton requested both Bradley and Eisenhower visit as soon as possible. They did so on 12 April, the same day of the salt mine visit. In a scene recorded by Lieutenant Moore, Eisenhower, Patton and Bradley were shown a pit in which the bodies of prisoners would be burned or buried. Such prisoners died from illness, exhaustion, brutality and murder. Their guide professed to be an inmate but Eisenhower thought otherwise due to his healthy appearance. The guide was discovered the following day, having been killed apparently by former prisoners. All three generals left horrific descriptions of their experiences (Bradley, *A Soldier's Story*, 539–40; Patton, *War As I Knew It*, 276–7; Eisenhower, *Crusade in Europe*, 408–10). Bradley stated that more than 3,200 corpses lay in shallow graves; other prisoners sprawled dead in the streets. Eisenhower immediately requested press reporters selected at random and legislators from America and Britain visit this and many other camps discovered by the advancing Allies. The supreme commander wanted documentation of the unbelievable crimes, in anticipation of prosecutions, and should individuals in the future contend it was all a hoax perpetrated by the Allies for propaganda. That same evening Patton learned during a radio broadcast that President Roosevelt had died and so informed Bradley and Eisenhower. (*NARA*)

(**Above**) Myers recording a harrowing image on 11 April of rows of dead prisoners at Mittlebau-Dora Lager near Nordhausen in Thuringia. Roughly 1,300 dead were found in the camp when the 104th Division reached the location a few days earlier. However, most inmates had been evacuated as the Americans approached. The camp emerged in 1943 as a production area for V-2 rockets and was first populated by prisoners from Buchenwald. It initially used underground tunnels and chambers for manufacturing and rudimentary shelter but eventually above-ground barracks, a crematorium and other structures were constructed. Prisoners were kept in appalling conditions and sanitation was virtually non-existent. While precise accounting is not possible, inmates who died have been estimated around 20,000 or about one-third of those who laboured at the camp complex. (*NARA*)

(**Opposite, above**) These impressive images of a V-2 (*Vergeltung* for vengeance) rocket on a launch pad were removed from a German prisoner on 13 April, possibly at Mittlebau-Dora given the focus on V-2 production at the camp complex. (*NARA*)

(**Opposite, below**) Troops from the 1st Division were present in the Harz Mountains village of Zellerfeld, located between the larger cities of Hannover and Kassel. A woman watched her home burning on 13 April. (*NARA*)

Lindgrew saw two hungry refugees in Zellerfeld on the same day, 13 April. (*NARA*)

Ruins in Zellerfeld during occupation by First Army troops on 13 April. (*NARA*)

Troops from 101st Infantry in the 26th Division run past a flaming fuel cart in Kronach north-west of Bayreuth on 14 April. *(NARA)*

Hollander photographed troops from the 78th Division moving past the ruins of Remscheid north-east of Cologne in the Ruhr district on 15 April. The final reduction of the Ruhr and the defending troops was at hand. *(NARA)*

(**Opposite, above**) Pletcher observed Colonel Raff and Lieutenant Colonel Bennet (S-2 or intelligence officer) from the 507th Parachute Infantry receiving a 'receipt' for the city of Duisburg north of Düsseldorf in the Ruhr on 17 April. (*NARA*)

(**Opposite, above**) Payne photographed soldiers from the 17th Airborne raising an American flag over Duisburg on 20 April. (*NARA*)

(**Above**) Ornitz recorded the discovery of the painting 'Wintergarden' by Edouard Manet in an underground storage vault on 15 April. The painting had been removed from a museum in Berlin. (*NARA*)

(**Above**) Arnow witnessed recovery by the 101st Airborne of a painting purported to be 'Christ with the Woman Taken in Adultery' by Johannes Vermeer. It was photographed at Zell am See in the Austrian Tyrol on 21 April. Other works purchased or stolen by Hermann Göring were also present. In this case Göring had been fooled: this one was a forgery painted by Han van Meegeren. (*NARA*)

(**Opposite, above**) Ten supposed SS troops identified as having participated in the killings at Baunez crossroads near Malmédy were captured by Third Army near Passau. Blefer photographed the group on 7 May. (*NARA*)

(**Opposite, below**) The 82nd Airborne encountered Wöbbelin labour camp north of Ludwigslust and east of Hamburg in May. According to orders from Eisenhower, victims at such camps were to be buried or exhumed from mass pits and reburied in individual graves. Local German men would supply the labour whenever possible. All local citizens who could possibly do so were required to walk through the camps to witness the horror perpetrated in the name of the Nazi Party and more broadly the German people. The photographer Clemmer recorded several images at Wöbbelin on 7 May. Roughly 200 prisoners, all considered victims of starvation, were prepared for burial in graves marked with crosses unless other religious affiliations could be determined. (*NARA*)

Civilians were filing past, with at least one younger woman appearing defiant or resentful of the photographer. (*NARA*)

An elderly couple appeared stoic. (*NARA*)

German civilians file past the starved victims of Wöbbelin who were wrapped in sheets before burial. *(NARA)*

Chapter Six

Aftermath

The Western Allies pushed into the heart of Germany during April as Russian armies moved towards Berlin. Remarkable discoveries of stolen art were found in castles and salt mines. The inevitable results of Nazi racial, ethnic and religious hatred emerged in the horrors at numerous labour and extermination camps. The end came with the capitulation of Berlin and contact between Russian and American forces on the River Elbe. The Third Reich surrendered to the Allies in early May. Germany was divided into four zones of occupation and the mammoth task of retribution and reconstruction from the chaos of the Second World War began.

*   *   *

Europe in May 1945 was transformed from the previous year. Contrasts were evident between early 1944 with coiled springs east and west and September with breakthroughs and breakouts in eastern and north-west Europe. Nevertheless, the war would last through the fall and winter into the following spring due to a range of factors, particularly German resistance aided by easing of their logistical challenges as those of the Allies increased.

The geopolitical situation continued to improve for the Allies yet the origins of Cold War conflict and Soviet dominance of eastern Europe that defined the second half of the twentieth century emerged. In the east, Finland sought peace terms after the Soviets advanced against Army Group North. Romania abandoned the Axis alliance and switched sides following decimation of southern army groups and the Russian advance through Ukraine. Continued movement of the Red Army against Hungary had implications for the Balkans and south-eastern Europe.

The Western Allies found themselves on the border of Germany after rapid advance across France and Belgium following the breakout from Normandy. The invasion of the French Mediterranean coast in August and subsequent movement up the Rhône Valley placed further pressure on German defences in the west. The Allies faced logistical challenges and a strategic debate embedded in deeper controversies between American and British generals within the alliance. The misadventure of Operation Market Garden in Holland in September required air transport capacity needed to supply the advance on other portions of the front. The failure of the offensive, marked by some of the most desperate and heroic fighting yet seen, was all the more tragic for the prolonged suffering of the Dutch population.

The American Army entered Germany near Aachen in September but became entangled in bitter and very costly fighting in the Hürtgen Forest through November. As early as September, Hitler decided a surprise offensive in the west might separate the Allied armies, recapture the crucial supply port of Antwerp and possibly permit transfer of much-needed forces back to the Russian front by early 1945. The Ardennes offensive launched in mid-December decimated the German Army in the west, but also cost the United States more soldiers than any battle in her history.

Following the capture of Rome in June 1944, mountainous terrain, German resistance, and a shifting focus to north-west Europe combined to relegate the Italian Campaign to secondary status. Still, Allied and German troops continued to struggle and die. Edward Wright, who offered much insight during his correspondence with Wendall Wilkie, was killed in Tuscany on 13 July. His unit – 2nd Battalion, 350th Infantry of the 88th Division – would later sustain 50 per cent casualties after being surrounded on a hilltop in September. By the spring of 1945 the Allies pushed up to the Austrian border and prepared to enter central Europe from the south.

Four years after the end of hostilities, a farmer near Affler, Germany, encountered the grave of an American soldier. First Lieutenant John Leary, who enabled his men from the 513th Parachute Infantry to withdraw under enemy fire in February 1945, was no longer missing in action.[1] His remains were initially interred in Belgium before repatriation to his widow and two young children on Staten Island, New York.

Another soldier who did not survive to revel in the end of the war was the best friend of the 1st Battalion, 502nd Parachute Infantry – Squadron Sergeant Major James 'Paddy' McRory of the Irish Guards. The tank commander who provided considerable material and morale assistance to the battalion in Holland was killed on the north German plain on 24 April 1945 and buried in the Becklingen War Cemetery.

The Red Army entered territory of Axis ally Hungary and pre-war German soil along the Baltic in the fall of 1944. Their brutality towards civilian populations in Budapest and East Prussia offered a precursor of suffering in the heart of Germany and no doubt stiffened both German resolve to resist and the Soviet thirst for revenge. Josef Stalin and the Soviet high command at Stavka were determined to drive into the Reich and be the first to enter Berlin.

The sacrifice and success of the Allies in their advance across north-west Europe and in Italy are in no way diminished by recognition of what many considered the essential contribution of soldiers from Russia and numerous eastern European and Asian lands in destruction of the Third Reich. Plans for the invasion of Germany were devised in the fall of 1944 and discussed with the principal army front commanders. Stalin encouraged competition among his senior field commanders, which now included Georgiy Zhukov who had been placed in command of First Belorussian

Front. Stalin decreed this front would capture Berlin, to the intense annoyance of Ivan Koniev and First Ukrainian Front. Then, as the advance was underway in April 1945, Stalin deliberately permitted Koniev to move towards the German capital, perhaps to spur – or punish – Zhukov.

Whatever the reason, First Belorussian Front entered the city in late April and accepted its surrender on 2 May.[2] By then Hitler and Joseph Goebbels and his family were dead. The camel Kuznechik who pulled an ammunition cart across eastern Europe and survived wounds at Stalingrad was led by his handler through the shattered city to spit on the Reichstag. The campaign to subjugate Berlin cost the Red Army 78,000 casualties and more than 304,000 if all three advancing fronts are considered.[3]

American and Russian troops made contact at Torgau on the River Elbe on 25 April. The Nazi regime had essentially fallen but the war continued for another two weeks. Among the forces that pushed past Berlin to the south was Nikolai Belov. His journal recorded the misery of a winter spent in front line trenches and expectations for the coming offensive. He was wounded in Belorussia during the great Destruction of Army Group Centre in the summer of 1944 and sent home to his wife Lidiya before returning for the final campaign. On 5 May Belov was killed on the Elbe, three days before the formal end of the war.[4]

Vasily Grossman also returned to the Red Army in the winter of 1945, to cross a partially destroyed bridge into the ruins of Warsaw. Grossman served as a reporter for the army newspaper *Krasnaya Zvezda* (Red Star) and entered Treblinka extermination camp in the summer of 1944. Overcome by the experience, he left the front for a time. Once he returned, Grossman remained with the army to report on its advance into Germany and ultimately witness the physical and human devastation of Berlin. Many residents but particularly women found no mercy among soldiers of the Red Army. Doctors and clinics reported tens of thousands of women raped during April and early May in Vienna and Berlin.[5] (By comparison, American military authorities in Germany documented 402 allegations of rape in April and 501 in May 1945, most of which would be substantiated in court proceedings. There was some suspicion actual instances were greater than the number documented.)[6]

Red Army soldiers were stunned by the material prosperity encountered from East Prussia to Berlin. Paved roadways, prosperous farms and suburban homes with electrical fixtures and indoor plumbing led them to ask why the Wehrmacht invaded Russia in the first place.[7]

One thing the Germans created was radical change in the human landscape. Judt described the long-term result of the Nazi programme in central and eastern Europe as 'social levelling' where removal of Jews and minorities enabled others in the local population to assume vacated roles in society. The Nazi programme consisted of three elements: destruction of Jews and all other educated members of the population in Poland and the western Soviet Union; descent of surviving local Slavs into a base form of serfdom; settlement of ethnic Germans on the vacant lands.[8]

Three Cities

The tales of three cities reflect the extremes of outcomes Europeans would experience. Rome was an Axis capital but survived due to limited Allied bombing, willingness of Hitler to preserve more than 2,000 years of architectural heritage, the presence of the Vatican, and relatively early withdrawal of Italy from the war.

Paris escaped virtually unscathed although the impact on the civilian population was greater. The City of Light did not become a 'field of ruins' as Hitler desired, in spite of the many explosives placed on bridges and iconic structures of French heritage. Her survival resulted from a happy coincidence of the Normandy breakout, a limited number of German troops and rapid movement of Allied forces – particularly French ones – once Roger Gallois revealed destruction seemed imminent. The timing of the reaction on the part of the resistance was another important factor. Had the rising occurred in late July or early August, the outcome may have been much more tragic.

The reluctance of the German commander Dietrich von Cholitz and interventions of Pierre Charles Taittinger and the Swedish consul Raoul Nordling were factors that preserved the city. In particular, Cholitz is traditionally viewed as withstanding tremendous pressures including threats to his family's wellbeing to avoid initiating destruction of one of the world's great cities. Some historians disagree with this image of Cholitz, pointing to his earlier actions in August against the resistance and transcripts of phone conversations with OKW.[9]

It is also clear that despite German views of France as a traditional enemy, their occupation – though often violent – lacked the fundamental ideological and racist components underlying virtually all of their actions in the east. Jewish citizens remained victims of ideology and were subject to deportation and murder.

Warsaw stood in stark contrast to the western capitals and indeed to other cities in the war. It was here the terrible consequences of Third Reich racial policies were given free rein to destroy the physical city and much of her population. Poland stood between two ruthless enemies that partitioned the country following the cynical non-aggression pact between the Nazis and Soviets.

What Poland in general and Warsaw in particular experienced was repeated in eastern and south-eastern Europe on smaller scales from 1941 onward. German troops that unleashed their fury in Warsaw in 1943 and 1944 had learned their trades further to the east with destruction of villages in Ukraine, Belorussia and western Russia. This brutality was frequently associated with the presence of racially driven formations such as the 1st SS Panzer Division and even more extreme groups such as the psychopaths and sadists with Dirlewanger and Kaminski. Regular army units were capable of brutal acts although some protested the indifference to civilian starvation in eastern Europe during the winter of 1941–42.[10]

When the more extreme SS units transferred to the west, fanaticism of some leaders and troops was unleashed in actions such as the destruction of Oradour-sur-Glane by 2nd SS Panzer Division in June 1944 and numerous murders of civilians and soldiers in the Ardennes by 1st SS in December 1944. Joachim Peiper and the division had been implicated in or undertook destruction of villages in Russia and Italy, the latter at Boves in September 1943 when the village was burned and twenty-two men killed in reprisal for the capture of two soldiers.[11] Such incidents occurred many times in eastern Europe and the Balkans.

Wehrmacht soldiers received gifts of bread and salt and were lauded as liberators in Belorussia and Ukraine until the reality of the Nazi racist programme began to emerge. Once the Germans had been driven out, the Soviets found the devastated social landscape much to their advantage.[12] Stalin clearly hoped to extend Soviet control into Poland. To that end, territory along the eastern border would be removed from Polish sovereignty and a 'Polish' central government servile to Moscow was created as an alternative to the government-in-exile in London.

German resolve to obliterate Warsaw would have been largely thwarted had Red Army troops entered the city shortly after arriving east of the Vistula in late July and early August 1944. Indeed, their approach was a major impetus propelling the Home Army into rising. First Belorussian Front sustained a beating at the hands of assembled German panzer divisions during the first week of August. Once crossings of the Vistula to the south and the Narew to the north were secured, the strategic importance of Warsaw was reduced. In addition, the Soviets were likely to be no more eager to assume the burden of feeding the inhabitants of Warsaw than the Allies had been to feed citizens in Paris while chasing the Germans across northern France.

Nevertheless, Stalin for his manifold ruthlessness was a skilled politician with an increasing interest in directing the future of postwar Europe. First Belorussian Front remained a powerful formation and additional Soviet reserves could have been assembled to drive back the Germans. Stalin was aware of the possible consequences of Warsaw being liberated by the Home Army and would not tolerate a free and democratic Poland on the border with the Soviet Union.

In any event, he was eager for the Germans to destroy the Home Army rather than face that army's opposition at a later date. A man who could approve execution of hundreds of Polish officers at Katyn, consistently lie about Soviet involvement by blaming the Germans, and respond to justified accusations by breaking relations with the Polish government-in-exile could easily find excuses for the Red Army to halt just east of Warsaw.

* * *

Strange ideas floated around as the end of war in Europe approached. James Gavin mentioned a conversation with General Brian Horrocks who predicted Britain would be finished with the end of empire and would be best served by forming a close alliance with the United States. Secretary of the Treasury Henry Morganthau, convinced fighting two wars against Germany was quite enough, proposed reducing the nation to an agrarian society to eliminate any industrial capacity for waging war. The idea may have initially been supported by Roosevelt but opposed by Churchill. Ed Wright was closer to the mark in his correspondence with Wilkie when he observed most soldiers expected the postwar period to be a close run competition between America and Russia for dominance.

Events took a different turn with Germany and Austria divided between the four powers, each of whom had districts in Berlin and Vienna under their control. The occupations ended in Austria during the 1950s but Berlin and eastern Germany remained under communist control and became flashpoints during the Cold War. Since Poland lost territory on her eastern frontier, the national border shifted westward to incorporate lands formerly German. Ethnic Germans were driven from or relocated out of Poland and western Czechoslovakia. American Third Army troops entered Pilsen before the end of the war but withdrew to the west in accordance with the agreed boundary between Allied armies.

The Moral Dimension

Does potential for such evil and capacity for such cruelty as manifested in the Second World War reside within each society? The Nazis were shrewd judges of the weaker aspects of human nature and knew how to exploit those failings. However, their racial and ethnic prejudices and mistreatments led populations initially regarding them as liberators to turn against their occupiers.

Waffen-SS soldiers killed eighty-six American soldiers near Malmédy in December 1944. American soldiers refused to accept the surrender of some German soldiers and considered killing others once they had surrendered in Normandy. The Gestapo executed members of the resistance throughout France. The French resistance killed Germans and some collaborators during the liberation of Paris and refused to accept surrenders at certain locations. While the scale of these behaviours clearly matters in an absolute sense, we still need to consider actions from a moral perspective.

Military and civilian leadership play decisive roles in such matters, particularly in the killing of prisoners and civilians. Just as leaders may inspire individuals to positive or heroic deeds, so may they motivate those who murder through racial, ethnic or religious hostility. It is both relevant and just to recognize that failures of American leadership would occur both before and after terrible incidents at No Gun Ri in Korea and Mỹ Lai in Vietnam.

The 2nd SS perpetrated horrific civilian crimes at Tulle and Oradour-sur-Glane in France and the 1st SS killed more than one hundred civilians in Belgium during the Ardennes offensive. The Nazi position on partisans and civilians who 'supported' them became clear during the war: any resistance was to be punished through executions and reprisals against local towns. Hubert Meyer, a former commander in the 12th SS Panzer Division, justified killings of eighty-six civilians in Ascq in northern France prior to Normandy as an inevitable result of non-traditional warfare. He protested vehemently the 1949 executions of two former leaders in the division for the murder of Canadian soldiers in Normandy, citing support from Basil Liddell Hart and others.[13]

The Nürnberg Tribunal was held from November 1945 to October 1946. The primary court trial considered the guilt of numerous officials in the military and civilian government of the Third Reich concerning charges that included instigating war and crimes against humanity. Whatever the legal complications such as convictions for crimes that did not previously exist, Nürnberg was an unprecedented effort to punish evil on an unprecedented scale. John Keegan noted the judgement of history has favoured the goals and outcomes of the trials, at least in countries occupied by or fighting against the Axis.[14]

Testimony offered and letters presented at Nürnberg documented the systematic Nazi programme to erode trust in or abolish an impartial judiciary, independent press and traditional religion while beginning active assault on Jewish citizens and certain minority groups. Political conservatism and overt or latent anti-Semitism meant the Nazis received collaboration from certain quarters in Vichy France and occupied countries.

During the trials, Albert Speer commented on use of foreign workers in war production and treatment of Hungarian Jews. Jürgen Stroop who prepared photo albums for Heinrich Himmler entitled 'The Jewish Residential quarter in Warsaw has ceased to exist!' described the May 1943 liquidation of the Warsaw ghetto. The former SS colonel Kurt Becher testified to killings of Jews at Mauthausen labour camp in 1944 and 1945 under orders from SS leader Ernst Kaltenbrunner. Others described V-rocket production at camps in Thuringia including Nordhausen using forced labour. As late as 25 April 1945 Becher was informed Kaltenbrunner expected at least 1,000 inmates to die each day at Mauthausen.[15]

Seven defendants were punished by prison terms from ten years to life, three were acquitted and two were ultimately not charged. Another twelve received death sentences and most were hanged on 16 October 1946, including Kaltenbrunner, Wehrmacht OKW leaders Alfred Jodl and Wilhelm Keitel, and Foreign Minister Joachim von Ribbentrop. Hermann Göring swallowed poison on the evening before his scheduled execution.

Martin Bormann was not present during the tribunal since his whereabouts were unknown. Most of the Allies were convinced he died trying to escape Berlin but the Americans devoted considerable effort to his capture. John Kormann was assigned to the 970th Counter-Intelligence Corps detachment in Berlin at the end of the war. Fluent in German, Kormann descended into the sewers of the city to look for fugitive Nazis, especially Bormann. He recovered a plaque dedicating a portion of an underground bunker to Hitler. At one point he reached a fixed iron grate and heard German voices coming from beyond the barrier. An entire regiment of United States infantry was sent into the sewers but found only refugees escaping from the Russian occupation area.

CIC analyses three years later concluded Bormann died in the city in May 1945 and was likely interred in a mass grave along Schönebergerstrasse near the Landswehr-kanal.[16] There the matter seemed to rest, so to speak, although supposed sightings continued in the 1940s and one FBI agent encountered someone resembling Bormann along Route 301 in southern Maryland during the 1960s.

In reality Bormann died on 2 May 1945 near the Lehrter railroad station – a different location than the CIC determination – in the company of numerous individuals attempting to escape from the Führer bunker following the death of Hitler. In 1963 Albert Krumnow informed police he assisted in the burial of two individuals on 8 May 1945 along Invalidenstrasse near the train station. An accidental discovery in 1972 of human remains very close to the supposed burials stimulated renewed interest. Genetic testing in 1998 eventually confirmed initial forensic analyses: the remains included those of Martin Bormann.

Many other trials were conducted to evaluate the extent of guilt and determine punishment for persons considered war criminals. These included members of the administration of labour and extermination camps such as Belzec, Dachau, Treblinka and Majdanek. Countries including those within the Soviet Bloc sought retribution.

A former commandant of Auschwitz named Rudolph Höss was convicted and hanged near the crematorium at the camp in April 1947. Others were tried in Kraków in late 1947 and executed or imprisoned for their actions at the camp complex. The testimony of Höss at Nürnberg was chilling in the dispassionate description of brutal camp conditions and murder of so many innocent people. By his estimate approximately 2.5 million inmates were gassed and burned with another 500,000 or so succumbing to disease or starvation. A shipment of 400,000 Hungarian Jews in the summer of 1944 was given particular mention.[17]

Charles MacDonald commanded a company in the 23rd Infantry of 2nd Division in the Ardennes and had as much right to despise the Teutonic enemy as anyone in the army. As a historian however, he admired their stalwart commitment to duty and argued for their generally correct behaviour except in a few instances. Malmédy was one of those exceptions.

The Allies at Nürnberg emphasized the principle of higher criminal responsibility for issuing or following illegal orders. Americans had a particular interest in punishing those responsible for the murders of soldiers near Malmédy and Honsfeld and civilians at several locations. Beyond members of Kampfgruppe Peiper believed to have actually shot the prisoners, commanding officers Sepp Dietrich and Fritz Kraemer from Sixth Panzer Army and Joachim Peiper were among dozens placed on trial. Most including Kraemer received prison terms of varying lengths while Dietrich and Peiper were among those sentenced to death.

The sentences were appealed and methods of American interrogation used to elicit apparent confessions called into question. The US Senate conducted an inquiry that conservative Senator Joe McCarthy first sought to dominate then abruptly left in protest. Ultimately Dietrich and Peiper were released after serving terms in prison. Public hostility to persons such as Peiper – likely reflecting passing of older Germans and emergence of the postwar generation – led the family to move to Alsace where he earned a living translating books. A leftist newspaper revealed his true identity and in July 1976 – while his family was away evidently due to threats – Peiper died when his home was set ablaze by fire bombs.[18]

Perspectives

John Keegan recognized the fundamental importance of a moral dimension and judgment. In the final analysis, the events we have been considering cannot be understood through lines on maps but as human tragedies. Losses in military battles and campaigns numbered in the hundreds to hundreds of thousands but the impacts to populations military and civilian require expansion of scale to the millions. Dislocations and resettlements after the war in addition to liberation of camps led to wandering groups of homeless including orphans across the continent. America was spared physical devastation but not civilian grief.

Why are these things remembered? Certainly a responsibility to honour the victims is often mentioned. Clearly there is a desire to prevent – or seek to prevent – the events from happening again. Yet violence and war crimes in the former Yugoslavia during the 1990s marked a return to the hatreds of the 1940s once communist control collapsed. Perhaps many feel a deeper need for a connection to the past and a sense of empathy – from a safe distance. The British scholar Paul Richards argued for the importance of 'a just and lasting peace' and we may regard remembrance and memorialization as potential elements of such a peace. It is critically important to recognize, however, that such remembrance may change through time to suit needs and concerns in the present.

One of the themes in this series has been the degree to which needs in the present direct interpretations of the past. Perhaps no issue illustrates this point more forcefully than denial of the Holocaust. Pierre Vidal-Naquet brilliantly defined the issue when he described denial as 'an attempt at extermination on paper that pursues in another register the actual work of extermination. One revives the dead in order the better to strike the living.'[19]

Despite extensive documentation – oral, written including eyewitness accounts, and photographic – of the existence of extermination camps and the survival of such camps as standing memorials (Auschwitz) or underground sites (Treblinka), those who deny the actions persist. These denials take many forms and the arguments are complex and seemingly versatile. Many espouse them not due to fundamental concerns with memories because the supporting historical data are extensive and compelling. Rather, their support is frequently rooted in modern prejudices: geopolitical, religious or racial.

A veteran who became an esteemed writer and professor – Paul Fussell – came to recognize that the evil of civilian abuse and murder on a massive scale provided Eisenhower, Churchill and others with a winning hand when it came to motivation for the final push through Germany.[20] The Allied soldiers had no need of reminders later, for many of them would never forget their first encounters with camps in April 1945 or even earlier in the east. At least they came to understand why the war had been fought.

Britain was not finished after the war, but many in the country continue to value the 'special relationship' with America. Challenges exist in defining Britain's relations with the European – largely western European – community of nations. France, Britain, Canada and America – whatever disagreements exist – will always have Normandy and the liberation. President Emmanuel Macron recognized that the French understood their freedom was owed to the veterans including a few hardy souls to whom he spoke at the Normandy American Cemetery in June 2019.

Many nations faced challenges addressing the collaboration of their own citizens. Existence of the government in Vichy and the extent to which authorities undertook arrest and deportation of their citizens, often but not exclusively Jewish, highlighted the challenges. The *épuration* or purge was the French answer but as in other countries was unevenly applied. The longer one avoided prosecution for wartime activities, the chances for more lenient sentences or none at all increased. One who did not escape retribution was Robert Brasillach who moved beyond anti-Semitic writings to denounce Jewish citizens and occupation opponents. Despite support from members of the literary community troubled by legal sentences for expression of views, even abhorrent ones, he was executed in February 1945.[21]

Germany's path to reconciliation has been long. During the five or ten years following the war, many government agencies were staffed by large numbers of Nazi Party members. More than half of the foreign ministry personnel in West Germany were former SS or Gestapo. In 1952 a poll revealed 37 per cent of West Germans thought an absence of Jews would be good for the country.[22]

The diary maintained by Victor Klemperer of his wartime experiences as the Jewish husband of an Aryan woman in Dresden revealed instances when older residents would come up and apologize for what happened to Germany. Young men, no doubt reflecting training in the Hitler Youth, at times with older men were more vicious in their treatment.[23] However, Germany has done much to educate postwar generations about the evils of political extremism, intolerance and hatred of those who may look or behave differently. The contrasting power of educational institutions and governments to advocate tolerance or indoctrinate intolerance has rarely been as clearly demonstrated.

Monuments and commemorations provide reminders of the past and warnings for the future. Efforts to inform residents in many European cities – Paris, Berlin, Vienna and Kraków to name but a few – of deportations and murder rooted in hatred provide important bridges between past and present. Many were eager to forget the legacy of division between east and west in Germany, but dedicated researchers identify and preserve traces of the Berlin Wall – the ultimate Cold War icon – as material reminders on the landscape of an ideological conflict. Archaeology has a role to play also in the identification of material remains such as military fortifications and entrenchments.[24] However, a former colleague who specialized in geo-archaeology is also the child of former inmates at Auschwitz. During a visit with other children of survivors, he noticed an eroding deposit appearing to hold bone fragments and wondered about geologic formation processes. He was gently informed by another traveller such places were not to be disturbed.

The restoration of democracy and liberty was certainly no small matter and remains the legacy of 1944 and 1945 in western and central Europe. It is ironic indeed that seventy-five years after the war Germany and France have become the strongest economic and political voices on the continent while the Western Allies remain concerned over the global aspirations of China and Russia, former allies in the struggle against the Axis. As nationalism or nativism seems to be growing within both former Allied and Axis countries, it is reasonable to question if the lessons of history are being ignored or misinterpreted. The 'just and lasting' peace advocated by Paul Richards seems more fragile than in past decades.

(**Opposite, above**) The 44th Division in Seventh Army marched through Imst, Austria, west of Innsbruck, on 8 May, VE Day. Weintraub, who recorded photographs in Normandy from early June onwards, was present to witness the scene. The 71st Infantry in the division fought an engagement a few days earlier at the nearby Fern Pass in the Tyrol (MacDonald, *The Last Campaign*, 469–71). (*NARA*)

(**Opposite, below**) Poinsett, another photographer who travelled across Europe with American forces, photographed a *Jagdpanzer* IV at the Skoda plant in Pilsen, Czechoslovakia, on 10 May. (*NARA*)

(**Above**) Survivors of Amphing in Germany were photographed by Mallinder on 4 May as the camp was liberated by Third Army. (*NARA*)

(**Opposite, above**) An aerial view of devastation in Wesel on the Rhine in March 1945, photographed by Major Trimble in a P-38 from the 363rd Tactical Reconnaissance Group. (*NARA*)

(**Opposite, below left**) The grave of Warrant Officer and Squadron Sergeant Major James McRory of the Irish Guards killed in April 1945 and buried in Becklingen War Cemetery in Germany. (*CWGC*)

(**Opposite, below right**) First Lieutenant John Leary from New York and the 513th Parachute Infantry was declared missing leading a patrol across the border into Germany in early February 1945. His burial location was discovered by a German farmer four years later and he was ultimately returned to the United States. (*Lillian and John Leary*)

This 1948 sketch in a 970th Counter-Intelligence Corps Detachment memorandum indicated a mass grave location in Berlin that supposedly held the remains of Martin Bormann. A chance discovery in 1972 of human remains at a different location near the Lehrter train station uncovered his actual grave. *(NARA)*

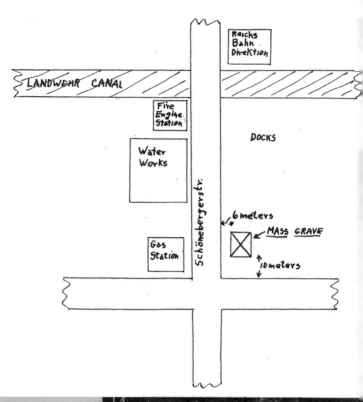

Adam Josef Westhoff testified on 11 April 1946 during the investigation of Wilhelm Keitel at the Nürnberg Tribunal. Keitel as nominal commander of the OKW endorsed Hitler's 1942 order for the execution of commandos and was found guilty of sanctioning the killing of soldiers and political prisoners. He was hanged on 16 October 1946. *(NARA)*

Survivors of the December 1944 massacre south of Malmédy in Belgium gathered in the field near the Baunez crossroads on 9 April 1946. *(NARA)*

Two survivors of the massacre – Private Samuel Dobyns and another soldier named Wolf – joined the group who returned to the Baunez crossroads on 9 April. *(NARA)*

(**Above**) Fritz Kraemer (standing) served as chief of staff for Sixth Panzer Army during the Ardennes offensive. The former Brigadeführer was among seventy-four defendants tried for the murders of American soldiers and Belgian civilians during the offensive. Joachim Peiper was seated to the left of Kraemer. (*NARA*)

(**Opposite, above**) Investigators also visited the nearby town of Honsfeld to examine the apparent locations of the murder of American prisoners in December 1944. (*NARA*)

(**Opposite, below**) A plaque to 101st Airborne on a wall in the square of Sainte-Marie-du-Mont celebrating liberation of the Norman town.

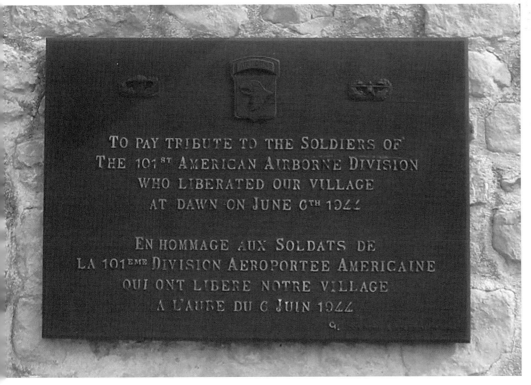

TO PAY TRIBUTE TO THE SOLDIERS OF
THE 101ST AMERICAN AIRBORNE DIVISION
WHO LIBERATED OUR VILLAGE
AT DAWN ON JUNE 6TH 1944

EN HOMMAGE AUX SOLDATS DE
LA 101EME DIVISION AEROPORTEE AMERICAINE
QUI ONT LIBERE NOTRE VILLAGE
A L'AUBE DU 6 JUIN 1944

LES FORCES ALLIEES
DEBARQVENT SVRCETTE
PLAGE QV-ELLES NOMMEN
OMAHA BEACH et LIBEREN
L'EVROPE · 6 JVIN 1944

THE ALLIED FORCES
LANDING ON THIS
SHORE WHICH THEY CAL
OMAHA BEACH LIBERAT
EVROPE · JVNE 6TH 1944

A sweeping Art Deco monument erected by the French at Exit D-3 on Omaha Beach.

A statue to 29th Division that commemorates all amphibious infantry was recently placed behind Dog Green sector of Omaha Beach.

View facing west across the narrow River Merderet to Cauquigny. The adjacent meadows were flooded in June 1944. An elevated causeway contested for several days at the beginning of the invasion is located behind the trees along the left edge.

Members of the resistance in Paris defend the Pont Neuf across the Seine during the liberation of the city in August 1944. *(NARA)*

The Pont Neuf on a more peaceful August day fifty-seven years later.

The bridges over the Seine within and beyond Paris were important strategic prizes for both Allies and Germans.

(**Left**) A plaque in the Gare de l'Est in Paris asks that French citizens deported to extermination camps never be forgotten. More than 70,000 Jewish residents including 11,000 children were sent to the camps; only 2,500 survived. (**Right**) A sign commemorating the fiftieth anniversary of Operation Market Garden placed on a wall in Nijmegen.

DE 1942 À 1944
PLUS DE 70 000 JUIFS DE FRANCE,
DONT 11 000 ENFANTS, ONT ÉTÉ DÉPORTÉS
DES GARES DE DRANCY, BOBIGNY, COMPIÈGNE,
PITHIVIERS ET BEAUNE-LA-ROLANDE
VERS LES CAMPS D'EXTERMINATION NAZIS.
SEULS 2500 D'ENTRE EUX ONT SURVÉCU.
N'OUBLIONS JAMAIS.
LES FILS ET FILLES DES DÉPORTÉS JUIFS DE FRANCE.

TO COMMEMORATE
THE 50TH ANNIVERSARY
OPERATION MARKET GARDEN

17TH SEPT. 1944   17TH SEPT. 1994

WE WILL REMEMBER THEM

On the stone:

AA

U.S. 82ND AIRB. DIV.
WAALCROSSING
20 SEPT. 1944
504 PARACHUTE INFANTRY
307 ENG.   376 PFABN
IN COÖP. WITH
505 PAR. INFANTRY
GUARDS ARMOURED DIV.

18 SEPT. 1984

HIER VOND
PLAATS
OP
20·9·1944
DE HELDHAFTIGE
OVERSTEEK
VAN DE WAAL

(**Above**) Stone stelae honour the 82nd Airborne Division troops who crossed the River Waal and the Guards Armoured Division who supported them on 20 September 1944. The stelae were placed to commemorate the fortieth anniversary of the crossing.

(**Opposite, above**) The highway bridge across the Waal in Nijmegen seized during the crossing as it appeared seventy years later.

(**Opposite, below**) A field near the Baunez crossroads massacre site in 1999.

The memorial wall at the Baunez crossroads to the American soldiers killed on 17 December 1944.

A plaque placed in September 1945 on the stone bridge across the River Amblève in Stavelot, Belgium, commemorated 131 citizens killed by 'les hordes Nazies' in December 1944.

A road bridge at this location in Trois-Ponts was destroyed by American engineers on 18 December 1944 after an anti-tank gun crew fired on the leading German tank. A plaque on the reconstructed bridge commemorates the gun crew and the 51st Engineer Combat Battalion whose actions caused such difficulties for Kampfgruppe Peiper. Another plaque to the left honours the memory of civilians murdered in the town.

The 'Voie de la Liberté' was created in the late 1940s to commemorate the Allied advance from Cherbourg and Sainte-Mère-Église in Normandy across France to Bastogne in Belgium. Concrete pylons placed at intervals of 1km on roads marked the general route of XX Corps. This monument, repainted before 1999, stood south of Bastogne on the main road from Arlon to mark a route used by III Corps during its movement to reach the besieged town in December 1944.

IN MEMORIUM TO OUR
COMRADES WHO FELL
WITH THE BRIDGE

276 TH ENGR (C) BN.

MAJ. JAMES E. FOLEY CAPT. RAYMOND F. BESNER
CAPT. WILLARD O. PABST 2D LT. GENE C. ENOS
2D LT. WILLIAM C. MILLER SGT. AUGUST ALBANI
SGT. ARTHUR BROWN SGT. LEONARD E. NEAL
TEC. 4 RALPH D. CAMPBELL TEC. 4 ED. D. SMOTHERMAN
CPL. NOBLE S. KIRKWOOD PFC. CLYDE HEAPS
PFC. JAMES R. PETTIS PFC. BEN. R. ROWLAND Jr.
PFC. JAMES E. BAGGETT PFC. QUITMAN GOAR
PFC. JOHN S. HAUF SR. PFC. JAMES E. HERRING
PFC. THELBERT E. ROBINETT PFC. LYLE W. HOFFMAN
PFC. KENNETH G. HOLLIS PVT. VESLEY L. LOWERY

American infantry and armour moved over the Ludendorff railroad bridge across the Rhine at Remagen before it collapsed due to damage sustained as the Germans sought to destroy the span. A plaque on one surviving tower commemorated the engineers who lost their lives when the bridge fell. Zitkus photographed the brother of Major James Foley, one of the engineers lost, standing near the plaque on 25 April 1945. (NARA)

A preserved section of the wall that enclosed the Jewish ghetto in Kraków, Poland, until the residents were killed or driven into camps in 1943. The image was recorded in 2004.

דא געלעבם.
געליםן און אומגעקומן
דורך די הענד פֿון די
היטלעריסטישע מערדער
פֿון האנען האם זיי געפֿירם
דער לעצמער וועג צו די
לאגערן פֿון אומקום
דער פֿראגמענם פֿון די ייִדיש
געטא-מויערן

TU ŻYLI, CIERPIELI
I GINĘLI Z RĄK
HITLEROWSKICH OPRAWCÓW.
STĄD WIODŁA ICH
OSTATNIA DROGA
DO OBOZÓW ZAGŁADY
FRAGMENT MURÓW
GETTA ŻYDOWSKIEGO
1941-1943

A plaque on the ghetto wall stating, 'Here they lived, suffered and died at the hands of Hitler's executioners. From here they led the last way to the extermination camps. Fragment of the walls of the Jewish Ghetto in 1941–1943.'

Image Credits

NB: Page numbers are in **bold**. Any images not credited are from the author's collection.

Chapter One: The Winter Offensive

18 NARA 111-SC-197697; **19** (top) NARA 111-SC-197699, (bottom) NARA 111-SC-197539; **20** (top) NARA 111-SC-197261, (bottom) NARA 111-SC-197739; **21** NARA 111-SC-197752; **22** (top) NARA 111-SC-197919, (bottom) NARA 111-SC-198177; **23** NARA 111-SC-197569; **24** (top) NARA 111-SC-198241, (bottom) NARA 111-SC-198250; **25** (top) NARA 111-SC-341648, (bottom) NARA 111-SC-341649; **26** NARA 111-SC-197561; **27** NARA 111-SC-341645; **28** (top) NARA 111-SC-341654 (bottom) NARA 111-SC-341658; **29** NARA 111-SC-198252; **30** (top) NARA 111-SC-333945, (bottom) NARA 111-SC-341661; **31** (top) NARA 111-SC-341630, (bottom) NARA 111-SC-341635; **32** NARA 111-SC-198244; **33** (top) NARA 111-SC-198468, (bottom) NARA 111-SC-198469; **34** NARA 111-SC-197755; **35** (top) NARA 111-SC-198302, (bottom) NARA 111-SC-198204; **36** NARA 111-SC-198188; **37** (top) NARA 111-SC-198305, (bottom) NARA 111-SC-198278; **38** (top) NARA 111-SC-199680; **39** NARA 111-SC-204209; **40** NARA 111-SC-197547; **41** (top) NARA 111-SC-198340, (bottom) NARA 111-SC-197557; **42** (top) NARA 111-SC-197564, (bottom) NARA 111-SC-410060; **43** (top) NARA 111-SC-198119, (bottom) NARA 111-SC-198120; **44** NARA 111-SC-198332; **45** NARA 111-SC-198115; **46** NARA 111-SC-198114; **47** (top) NARA 111-SC-226837, (bottom) NARA 111-SC-226653; **48** (top) NARA 111-SC-226891, (bottom) NARA 111-SC-226895; **49** NARA 111-SC-226667; **50** (top) NARA 111-SC-329977, (bottom) NARA 111-SC-198389; **51** NARA 111-SC-200560; **52** (top) NARA 111-SC-198403, (bottom) NARA 111-SC-415373; 53 (top) NARA 111-SC-198388, (bottom) NARA 111-SC-198304; **54** NARA 111-SC-198651; **55** (top) NARA 111-SC-198452, (bottom) NARA 111-SC-199295; **56** (top) NARA 111-SC-415374, (bottom) NARA 111-SC-198450; **57** NARA 111-SC-336334; **58** (top) NARA 111-SC-421334, (bottom) NARA 111-SC-198647; **59** NARA 111-SC-329953; **60** NARA 111-SC-198461; **61** (top) NARA 111-SC-377581, (bottom) NARA 111-SC-198523; **62** NARA 111-SC-197827.

Chapter Two: The Ardennes Winter

77 NARA 111-SC-198343; **78** NARA 111-SC-370944; **79** (bottom) NARA 111-SC-198524; **80** NARA 111-SC-370951; **81** (top) NARA 111-SC-198548, (bottom) NARA 111-SC-198642; **82** NARA 111-SC-246370; **83** (top) NARA 111-SC-198899, (bottom) NARA 111-SC-198719; **84** (top) NARA 111-SC-364283, (bottom) NARA 111-SC-253915; **85** NARA 111-SC-198793; **86** (top) NARA 111-SC-253916, (bottom) NARA 111-SC-229746; **87** NARA 111-SC-199109; **88** NARA 111-SC-199018; **89** (top) NARA 111-SC-421456; (bottom) NARA 111-SC-283728; **90** (top) NARA 111-SC-198849, (bottom) NARA 111-SC-370952; **91** NARA 111-SC-199155; **92** NARA 111-SC-199161; **93** (top) NARA 111-SC-199190; **94** (top) NARA 111-SC-370954, (bottom) NARA 111-SC-199214; **95** NARA 111-SC-198856; **96** (top) NARA 111-SC-199162, (bottom) NARA 111-SC-199157; **97** NARA 111-SC-199344; **98** (top) NARA 111-SC-265224, (bottom) NARA 111-SC-370955; **99** NARA 111-SC-253918; **100** (top) NARA 111-SC-248304, (bottom) NARA 111-SC-199378; **101** NARA 111-SC-265513; **102** (top) NARA 111-SC-199031, (bottom) NARA 111-SC-199057; **103** NARA 111-SC-326470; **104** (top) NARA 111-SC-199413, (bottom) NARA 111-SC-294660; **105** NARA 111-SC-199467; **106** NARA 111-SC-294658; **107** (top) NARA 111-SC-199228, (bottom) NARA 111-SC-199058; **108** NARA 111-SC-253919; **109** (top) NARA 111-SC-254009, (bottom) NARA 111-SC-377622; **110** (top) NARA 111-SC-535231, (bottom) NARA 111-SC-254002; **111** NARA 111-SC-198603; **112** (top) NARA 111-SC-390441, (bottom) NARA 111-SC-325603; **113** NARA 111-SC-198201; **114** NARA 111-SC-199145; **115** (top) NARA 111-SC-198768, (bottom) NARA 111-SC-198770; **116** (top) NARA 111-SC-198769, (bottom left) NARA 111-SC-199212, (bottom right) NARA 111-SC-199059; **117** NARA 111-SC-199422; **118** NARA 111-SC-199685; **119** (top) NARA 111-SC-198754, (bottom) NARA 111-SC-199150; **120** NARA 111-SC-198749; **121** (top) NARA 111-SC-199062, (bottom) NARA 111-SC-199414; **122** NARA 111-SC-329791; **123** (top) NARA 111-SC-199231, (bottom) NARA 111-SC-199651; **124** (top) NARA 111-SC-198608, (bottom) NARA 111-SC-199229; **125** NARA 111-SC-199103; **126** NARA 111-SC-325602; **127** (top) NARA 111-SC-199431, (bottom) NARA 111-SC-199663; **128** (top) NARA 111-SC-199676, (bottom) NARA 111-SC-199645; **129** NARA 111-SC-199647; **130** NARA 111-SC-199675; **131** (top) NARA 111-SC-199682, (bottom) NARA 111-SC-199634.

Chapter Three: Advance to the Rhine
139 NARA 111-SC-199789; **140** NARA 111-SC-268781; **141** (top) NARA 111-SC-200084, (bottom) NARA 111-SC-336751; **142** NARA 111-SC-332982; **143** (top) NARA 111-SC-201973, (bottom) NARA 111-SC-205685; **144** NARA 111-SC-203252; **145** (top) NARA 111-SC-203336, (bottom) NARA 111-SC-203339; **146** NARA 111-SC-203341; **147** (top) NARA 111-SC-329116, (bottom) NARA 111-SC-203345; **148** (top) NARA 111-SC-203329, (bottom) NARA 111-SC-203330; **149** (top) NARA 111-SC-203443, (bottom)NARA 111-SC-203444; **150** (top) NARA 111-SC-203445, (bottom) NARA 111-SC-203332; **151** NARA 111-SC-203333; **152** NARA 111-SC-203324; **153** (top) NARA 111-SC-203325, (bottom) NARA 111-SC-203335; **154** NARA 111-SC-203322.

Chapter Four: Varsity
168 NARA 111-SC-203299; **169** (top) NARA 111-SC-203298, (bottom) NARA 111-SC-203304; **170** (top) NARA 111-SC-253923, (bottom) NARA 111-SC-203300; **171** NARA 111-SC-253920; **172** NARA 111-SC-253924; **173** (top) NARA 111-SC-203396, (bottom) NARA 111-SC-203394; **174** NARA 111-SC-203303; **175** (top) NARA 111-SC-203397, (bottom) NARA 111-SC-202650; **176** NARA 111-SC-203230; **177** (top) NARA 111-203347, (bottom) NARA 111-203346; **178** (top) NARA 111-377623, (bottom) NARA 111-SC-203337; **179** (top) NARA 111-SC-203393, (bottom) NARA 111-SC-202655; **180** (top) NARA 111-SC-202656, (bottom) NARA 111-SC-202657; **181** NARA 111-SC-202658; **182** NARA 111-SC-202659; **183** (top) NARA 111-SC-253930, (bottom) NARA 111-SC-203236; **184** (top) NARA 111-SC-203240, (bottom) NARA 111-SC-203243; **185** NARA 111-SC-253933; **186** NARA 111-SC-203238; **187** (top) NARA 111-SC-203242, (bottom) NARA 111-SC-203237; **188** (top) NARA 111-SC-202652, (bottom) NARA 111-SC-202653; **189** (top) NARA 111-SC-203241, (bottom) NARA 111-SC-202651; **190** NARA 111-SC-202654; **191** (top) NARA 111-SC-253931, (bottom) NARA 111-SC-203232; **192** (top) NARA 111-SC-203432, (bottom) NARA 111-SC-203442; **193** NARA 111-SC-203441; **194** NARA 111-SC-203440; **195** NARA 111-SC-203437; **196** NARA 111-SC-203439.

Chapter Five: The Allies in Germany
203 (top) NARA 111-SC-204782, (bottom) NARA 111-SC-204783; **204** (top) NARA 111-SC-204673, (bottom) NARA 111-SC-253934; **205** (top) NARA 111-SC-254018, (bottom) NARA 111-SC-253935; **206** NARA 111-SC-204516; **207** NARA 111-SC-204519; **208** NARA 111-SC-203456;

209 (top left) NARA 111-SC-232840, (top right) NARA 111-SC-232839, (bottom) NARA 111-SC-206237; **210** (top) NARA 111-SC-206238, (bottom) NARA 111-SC-206239; 211 (top) NARA 111-SC-206235, (bottom) NARA 111-SC-206236; **212** (top) NARA 111-SC-231667, (bottom) NARA 111-SC-204680; **213** NARA 111-SC-203453; **214** NARA 111-SC-374666; **215** (top) NARA 111-SC-341511, (bottom) NARA 111-SC-265515; **216** (top) NARA 111-SC-265525, (bottom) NARA 111-SC-265527; **217** NARA 111-265530.

Chapter Six: Aftermath
229 (top) NARA 111-SC-204678, (bottom) NARA 111-SC-206649; **230** NARA 111-SC-206586; **231** (top) NARA 342-FH-3A22620, (bottom left) CWGC, (bottom right) Lillian and John Leary; **232** (top) NARA 319-Container 88 folder 2, (bottom) NARA 111-SC-234001; **233** (top) NARA 111-SC-233998, (bottom) NARA 111-SC-234004; **234** NARA 111-SC-240739; **235** (top) NARA 111-SC-234003; **238** (top) NARA 111-SC-193339; **244** NARA 111-SC-204920.

Notes

Chapter 1: The Winter Offensive

1. MacDonald, *Time for Trumpets*, 645–7; Zaloga, *Smashing Hitler's Panzers*.
2. Bennett, *Ultra in the West*, 191–204.
3. Leleu, *Waffen-SS*, tables 11 and 15.
4. 393rd A/A Report.
5. Cole, *Ardennes*, 100.
6. MacDonald, 378–80; 393rd A/A Report.
7. 9th Journal, 2100 17 December 1944; 23rd Journal, 2105 17 December 1944.
8. 9th Journal, 0245 18 December 1944 (message reported by 38th at 0200); 9th Journal, 0220 18 December 1944.
9. MacDonald, 395; Cavanagh, *Battle East of Elsenborn*.
10. 38th A/A Report, 3; MacDonald, 397–8.
11. Meyer, *12th SS Panzer II*, 271.
12. 23rd Journal, 1352 18 December 1944; 9th Journal, 1017 18 December 1944.
13. Meyer, 274–6.
14. 26th A/A Report, 3; MacDonald, 390.
15. 26th A/A Report, 3; 26th Journal, 1345 19 December 1944; MacDonald, 404.
16. 26th A/A Report, 4–5.
17. Meyer, 296–9. Companies 1 through 4 (Panthers) and companies 5 through 9 (Mark IVs) comprised the 12th SS divisional panzer regiment. An attached heavy Panzerjäger battalion contributed *Jagdpanther* units.
18. 26th A/A Report, 4–5; 26th Journal, 1635 21 December 1944.
19. 26th A/A Report, 5–6; Meyer, 304.
20. MacDonald, 198–210; Cavanagh, 69–70.
21. MacDonald, 222, 437–8; 'German Atrocities' 30th Division Periodic Report, 22 December 1944; Hansen diary, 24 December 1944.
22. Kennett, *G.I.*, 161.
23. MacDonald, 238–44.
24. Cole, 476–8; MacDonald, 527–9.
25. 326th Airborne Medical Company A/A Report 'Defense of Bastogne'; Hansen diary, 25 December 1944.
26. Third Army Bastogne and Saint-Vith Campaign, 3.
27. 'Notes on Bastogne Operation', 5; Bradley, *A Soldier's Story*, 472–3.
28. Patton, *War As I Knew It*, 175–7.
29. Hansen diary, 25 December 1944 (with reference to later events).
30. 120th A/A Report, December 1944; Munger interview, 22 December 2010.
31. Hansen diary, 19 December 1944.
32. Bradley, *A Soldier's Story*, 470.
33. Hansen diary, 31 December 1944.

Chapter 2: The Ardennes Winter

1. Dupuy, *Lion in the Way*; Cole, *Ardennes*; MacDonald, *Time for Trumpets*.
2. MacDonald, 468–75, 482–3.
3. 110th A/A Report, December 1944.
4. Cole, 212–37.
5. Cole, 247. The decoration awarded to Sergeant Willis was displayed in the hotel in the fall of 1999.
6. Cole, 253.
7. Cole, 238–58.
8. Gavin diary, 31 December 1944; Combat Interview (C. I.) Gavin 1945; Gavin, *On to Berlin*.
9. C.I. Gavin, 7–8; MacDonald, 448–9.
10. MacDonald, 562–84.
11. 513th A/A Report, 3; Patton, *War As I Knew It*, 203; 'Notes on Bastogne Operation', 4 January 1945.
12. 513th A/A Report, 4–5; 513th History.
13. Interview Company A/513th, 19 September 2010.
14. 'Notes on Bastogne Operation', 6–11; Third Army Bastogne and Saint-Vith Campaign, 7–8.
15. 506th Journal, 13–17 January 1945; Ambrose, *Band of Brothers*, 211–28.
16. MacDonald, 595–7; Montgomery, *Memoirs*, 284–6.
17. de Guingand, *Operation Victory*, 434–5.
18. MacDonald, 599.
19. Gavin diary, 14 January 1945.
20. MacDonald, 618.
21. A/A Reports for regiments mentioned.
22. *Nazi Conspiracy and Aggression, Vol. VI*, 686, 698–9, 717.

Chapter 3: Advance to the Rhine

1. Montgomery, *Memoirs*, 295.
2. Gavin diary, 18 January 1945.
3. Gavin diary, 10 February 1945 in Rott, Germany.
4. Horrocks, *Corps Commander*, 173–204.
5. Ellis, *Victory in the West, Vol. II*, 253–77.
6. Leary Citations, 14 May 1945 and 9 May 1950.
7. Third Army Eifel to the Rhine, 1–4.
8. Third Army Palatinate Campaign and Eifel to the Rhine.
9. Hansen diary, 7 March 1945.
10. Ellis, *Victory in the West, Vol. II*, 288–90.
11. Interview Company A/513th, 19 September 2010.
12. Gavin diary, 22 March 1945 at Sissons, France.

Chapter 4: Varsity

1. Bennett, *Ultra in the West*, 234.
2. 17th Airborne Historical Report, 1.
3. 1st Canadian Parachute Bn War Diary.
4. 8th Parachute Bn War Diary.
5. 9th Parachute Bn War Diary.
6. War Diaries for 5th Parachute Brigade and 7th, 12th and 13th Parachute Bns, 7th Bn Report 'Crossing the Rhine'.

7. 591st Parachute Sqd RE War Diary.
8. War Diaries for 6th Airlanding Brigade, 1st RUR, 2nd Ox Bucks and 12th Devons.
9. 6th Airlanding Brigade A/A Report.
10. 17th Airborne Historical Report; 507th Historical Report and Unit Journal.
11. 17th Airborne Historical Report, 1–4.
12. 194th Historical Report and Unit Journal.
13. Gavin diary, 25 March 1945.
14. Interview Company A/513th, 19 September 2010; Kormann interview, March and June 2013.
15. 195th, 224th and 225th Field Ambulance War Diaries and US 224th Parachute Medical Company A/A Report.
16. Ellis, *Victory in the West, Vol. II*, 291. The Pegasus Archive website counts around 8,705 men in 6th Airborne with 536 soldiers and 100 glider pilots listed as killed on 24–25 March. Divisional documents for the 17th Airborne record more than 10,000 men in the division.
17. Ellis, *Victory in the West, Vol. II*, 290–1; MacDonald, *The Last Offensive*, 313–4.
18. MacDonald, 313–4.
19. *Ibid.*

Chapter 5: The Allies in Germany
1. Bradley, *A Soldier's Story*, 535.
2. MacDonald, *The Last Offensive*, 386–99.
3. Third Army Forcing the Rhine to the Mulde.
4. Bennett, *Ultra in the West*, 257–63.
5. Third Army Crossing the Danube to Czechoslovakia and Austria.
6. Klemperer, *I Will Bear Witness*, 28–9, in Dresden first mentioned Auschwitz and Buchenwald in March 1942.
7. Hansen diary, 12 April 1945.
8. Gelhorn, 'Surely this War Was Made to Abolish Dachau'; Murrow, 'For Most of It I Have No Words'.
9. Interview Company A/513th, 19 September 2010; Kormann interview, March and June 2013.
10. Hansen diary, 12 and 13 April 1945.

Chapter 6: Aftermath
1. Leary Narrative Report, 18 May 1949.
2. Salisbury comments in *Zhukov's Greatest Battles*.
3. Beevor and Vongradova, *A Writer at War*, 273; Judt, *Postwar*, 18; Keegan, *Second World War*, 533.
4. Merridale, *Ivan's War*, 332–3.
5. Beevor and Vongradova; Judt, 20
6. Kennett, *G.I.*, 217–8. MacDonald, *The Last Offensive*, 333, reflected the same increase by evaluating cases brought to trial: 32 in January and February, 128 in March and 259 in April 1945.
7. Beevor and Vongradova, 341–2.
8. Judt, 36.
9. Freiburg archives, German/Arte source, 2011.
10. Terry, Ph.D. dissertation.
11. Westemeier, *Joachim Peiper*.
12. Judt, 36.
13. Meyer, *12th SS Panzer II*, 518–21.

14. Keegan, *Second World War*, 590. One Hungarian engineer in 1977 described the trials as 'the winners dictating to the losers' which they certainly were, but I asked him to consider the nature of the losers.
15. *Nazi Conspiracy and Agression, Vol. VI*, 450, 645, 773, 775–7.
16. 970th CIC memoranda, 18 May and 9 June 1948.
17. *Nazi Conspiracy and Aggression, Vol. VI*, 787–90. Modern calculations reduce the Höss estimate, by possibly 50 per cent.
18. MacDonald, *Time for Trumpets*, 620–23.
19. Vidal-Naquet, *Assassins of Memory*, 22.
20. Fussell, *The Boys' Crusade*, 162–5.
21. Riding, *And the Show Went On*, 321, 323–5.
22. Judt, 57–8.
23. Klemperer, *I Will Bear Witness*.
24. Cowell, 'Keeping Alive the Fading Memory of World War II'; Klausmeier, 'Mediation of an Uncomfortable Monument'; Schmidt, 'A Landscape of Memory'; Passmore and Harrison, 'Landscapes of the Battle of the Bulge'.

References

Army unit records, National Archives Record Group 407

Third US Army summary Bastogne and Saint-Vith Campaign and the Eifel to the Rhine December 1944 to March 1945 including 'Notes on Bastogne Operation' by General George Patton 16 January 1945.

Third US Army summary Palatinate Campaign, Forcing the Rhine to the Mulde, Crossing the Danube to Czechoslovakia and Austria March to May 1945.

'Burial of Victims of Nazi Atrocities', memorandum by order of General George Patton Third Army, 1 May 1945, based on memorandum from 12th Army Group, 21 April 1945.

17th Airborne Division Historical Report for Operation Varsity March 1945.

Memorandum by order of Major General William Miley, 17th Airborne Division, 27 March 1945.

'German Atrocities' 30th Infantry Division G-2 Periodic Report 22 December 1944, in 120th Infantry Journal file.

Combat Interview of Major General James Gavin 82nd Airborne Division Report on 'Bulge' Operation, interviewed March and April 1945 by Major J.F. O'Sullivan.

9th Infantry Unit Journal December 1944.

23rd Infantry Unit Journal December 1944.

26th Infantry After Action or A/A Report and Unit Journal December 1944.

38th Infantry A/A Report December 1944.

110th Infantry A/A Report December 1944.

120th Infantry A/A Report December 1944.

194th Glider Infantry History and Unit Journal March 1945.

224th Airborne Medical Company A/A Report 24–31 March 1945.

326th Airborne Medical Company A/A Report 'Defense of Bastogne' 17–28 December 1944.

393rd Infantry A/A Report December 1944.

464th Parachute Field Artillery Battalion A/A Report 24–31 March 1945.

506th Parachute Infantry Unit Journal December 1944–January 1945.

507th Parachute Infantry Historical Report and Unit Journal March–April 1945.

Company F and 3rd Battalion 507th Parachute Infantry A/A Reports 24 March 1945.

513th Parachute Infantry History 1942–1945, printed July 1945 in Vittel, France.

History of 513th Parachute Infantry, 11 June 1943–6 September 1945.

513th Parachute Infantry A/A Report Ardennes December 1944–February 1945.

Counter-Intelligence Corps files, National Archives Record Group 319

970th Counter-Intelligence Corps Detachment Berlin on apparent death and burial of Martin Bormann in May 1945, memoranda dated 18 May and 9 June 1948 (Container 88 folder 2).

British Army records

6th Airborne Division war diaries March–April 1945 (pegasusarchive.org):
  Brigades: 3rd and 5th Parachute and 6th Airlanding.

Parachute Battalions: 1st Canadian, 7th, 8th, 9th, 12th and 13th and 7th report 'Crossing the Rhine'.
Airlanding Battalions: 1st Royal Ulster Rifles, 2nd Oxfordshire and Buckinghamshire Light Infantry, 12th The Devonshire Regiment.
195th Airlanding and 224th and 225th Parachute Field Ambulance.
591st Parachute Battalion Royal Engineers.

Ambrose, S., *Band of Brothers. E Company, 506th Regiment, 101st Airborne from Normandy to Hitler's Eagle's Nest*, Simon and Schuster, New York, 1992.

Beevor, A. and Vongradova, L. editors and translators, *A Writer at War. Vasily Grossman with the Red Army, 1941–1945*. Pantheon Books, New York, 2005.

Bennett, R., *Ultra in the West. The Normandy Campaign of 1944–45*, Charles Scribner's Sons, New York, 1979.

Bradley, O., *A Soldier's Story*, Henry Holt and Company, New York, 1951.

Bryant, A., *Triumph in the West. Completing the War Diaries of Field Marshal Viscount Alanbrooke*, The Reprint Society, London, 1960 (first published by William Collins, 1959).

Campbell, W., *The Battle East of Elsenborn and the Twin Villages*, Pen & Sword, Barnsley, 2012 (first published by The Christopher Publishing Company, 1986).

Cole, H., *The Ardennes: Battle of the Bulge*, Office of the Chief of Military History, Washington DC, 1965.

Cowell, A., 'Keeping Alive the Fading Memory of World War II', *New York Times*, 24 June 2011.

de Guingand, F., *Operation Victory*, Charles Scribner's Sons, New York, 1947.

Dupuy, R.E., *St. Vith: Lion in the Way. The 106th Infantry Division in World War II*, Infantry Journal Press, Washington DC, 1949.

Edsel, R. and Witter, B., *The Monuments Men*, Center Street, New York, 2009.

Eisenhower, D., *Crusade in Europe*, Doubleday & Company, Garden City, 1948.

Ellis, L.F. with Warhurst, A.E., *Victory in the West, Volume II: The Defeat of Germany*, HMSO, London, 1968.

Freiburg Archives cited in German/Arte source, 2011.

Fussell, P., *The Boys' Crusade. The American Infantry in Northwestern Europe, 1944–1945*. The Modern Library/Random House, New York, 2003.

Gavin, J., diary December 1944–February 1945, US Army Military History Institute, Carlisle.

Gavin, J., *On to Berlin. Battles of an Airborne Commander 1943–1946*, The Viking Press, New York, 1984.

Gelhorn, M., 'Surely this War Was Made to Abolish Dachau', in *Reporting World War II, Part II: American Journalism 1944–1946*, 724–30, Library of America, New York, 1995 (originally published in *Collier's*, 23 June 1945).

Hansen, C., diary November 1944–May 1945, United States Army Military History Institute, Carlisle.

Horrocks, B. with Belfield E. and Essame H., *Corps Commander*, Charles Scribner's Sons, New York, 1977.

Hottelet, R., 'Big Jump into Germany', in *Reporting World War II, Part II: American Journalism 1944–1946*, 649–59, Library of America, New York, 1995 (originally published in *Collier's*, 5 May 1945).

Interview Company A 513th Parachute Infantry with Herb Anderson, Ed Ballas, Ralph Clarke, Hal Green, Robert Haight, Irv Hennings and Stanley Morrison, 19 September 2010.

Judt, T., *Postwar: A History of Europe Since 1945*. Penguin Books, New York, 2005.

Keegan, J., *Six Armies in Normandy: From D-Day to the Liberation of Paris*, Jonathan Cape Ltd, 1982, reprinted by Penguin Books Ltd, Harmondsworth, 1984.

Keegan, J., *The Second World War*, Penguin Books Random House, New York, 2016 (first published by Century Hutchinson, 1989).

Kennett, L., *G.I.: The American Soldier in World War II*, Charles Scribner's Sons, New York, 1987.

Klausmeier, A. 'Strategies for the Mediation of an Uncomfortable Monument: The Example of the Berlin Wall', in *On Both Sides of the Wall: Preserving Monuments and Sites of the Cold War Era*, edited by L. Schmidt and H. von Preuschen, 50–52, Westkreuz-Verlag, Berlin, 2005.

Klemperer, V., *I Will Bear Witness. A Diary of the Nazi Years 1942–1945*, translated by M. Chalmers, Random House, New York, 1999, original title *Ich will Zeugnis ablegen bis zum leitzten: Tagebücher 1933–1945 von Victor Klemperer*, Aufbau-Verlag GmbH, Berlin, 1995.

Kormann, J. interview 517th Airborne Signal Company, March and June 2013.

Leary, J., Citations for First Lieutenant John Leary for Silver Star 14 May 1945 and Bronze Star Medal 9 May 1950, in letter from the Adjutant General's Office, Records Administration Center, 9 May 1950 (courtesy of Lillian and John Leary).

Leary J., Narrative Report of Investigation and Disinterment Conducted at Affler, Germany, First Field Command, American Graves Registration Command, European Area, 18 May 1949 (courtesy of Lillian and John Leary).

Leleu, J.-L., *La Waffen-S.S. Soldats politiques en guerre.* Ouvrage publié avec le concours du Centre National des Lettres, Perrin, Paris, 2007.

MacDonald, C., *The Last Offensive*, Office of the Chief of Military History, Washington DC, 1973.

MacDonald, C., *A Time for Trumpets. The Untold Story of the Battle of the Bulge*, William Morrow and Company, Inc., New York, 1985.

Merridale, C., *Ivan's War: Life and Death in the Red Army, 1939–1945*, Metropolitan Books/Henry Holt and Company, New York, 2006.

Meyer, H., *History of the 12th SS Panzer Division Hitlerjugend, Vol. II*, J.J. Fedorwicz Publishing, Winnipeg, 1994, translated by H. Henschler, reprinted by Stackpole Books, Harrisburg, 2005.

MIAProject.net maintained by J.-P. Speder and J.-L. Seel, April 2019.

Montgomery, B., *The Memoirs of Field-Marshal the Viscount Montgomery*, World Publishing Company, Cleveland, 1958.

Munger, P. interview 120th Infantry 30th Division, 22 December 2010.

Murrow, E., 'For Most of It I Have No Words', in *Reporting World War II, Part II: American Journalism 1944–1946*, 681–5, Library of America, New York, 1995 (CBS Radio broadcast 15 April 1945).

Nazi Conspiracy and Aggression, Vol. VI, Office of United States Chief Counsel for Prosecution of Axis Criminality, Government Printing Office, Washington DC, 1946.

Passmore, D. and Harrison, P., 'Landscapes of the Battle of the Bulge: WW2 Field Fortifications in the Ardennes Forests of Belgium', *Journal of Conflict Archaeology*, 4, 87–107, Leiden, 2008.

Patton, G., *War As I Knew It*, Houghton Mifflin Company, New York, 1947, reprinted by Bantam Books, New York, 1979.

Riding, A., *And the Show Went On. Cultural Life in Nazi-Occupied Paris*, Vintage Books, New York, 2011 (originally published by Alfred Knopf, 2010).

Schmidt, L. 'The Berlin Wall: A Landscape of Memory', in *On Both Sides of the Wall: Preserving Monuments and Sites of the Cold War Era*, edited by L. Schmidt and H. von Preuschen, 11–17, Westkreuz-Verlag, Berlin, 2005.

Terry, N., 'The German Army Group Centre and the Soviet Civilian Population 1942–44', Ph.D. dissertation, King's College, London, 2006.

Vidal-Naquet, P., *Assassins of Memory. Essays on the Denial of the Holocaust*, translated by J. Mehlman, Columbia University Press, New York, 1992, original title *Les Assassins de la mémoire: 'Un Eichmann de papier et autres essais sur le révisionnisme'*, Éditions La Découverte, 1987.

Westemeier, J., *Joachim Peiper: A Biography of Himmler's SS Commander*, Schiffer Publications, Atglen, Pennsylvania, 2007.

Zaloga, S., *Smashing Hitler's Panzers*, Stackpole Books, Harrisburg, 2019.

Zhukov, G., *Marshal Zhukov's Greatest Battles*, edited by H. Salisbury and translated by T. Shabad, Harper & Row, New York, 1969.